Claire Macdonald and her husband run Kinloch Lodge Hotel on the Isle of Skye, which is also the family home for them and their four children. Claire is a well-known exponent of Scottish cooking and travels widely, lecturing and demonstrating recipes.

Claire
Macdonald
OF MACDONALD
Lunches

CORGI BOOKS

LUNCHES
A CORGI BOOK : 0 552 14428 2

Originally published in Great Britain by Doubleday,
a division of Transworld Publishers

PRINTING HISTORY
Bantam Press edition published 1996
Corgi edition published 1997

3 5 7 9 10 8 6 4

Set in Baskerville by
Hewer Text Composition Services, Edinburgh.

Corgi Books are published by Transworld Publishers,
61–63 Uxbridge Road, London W5 5SA,
a division of The Random House Group Ltd,
in Australia by Random House Australia (Pty) Ltd,
20 Alfred Street, Milsons Point, Sydney, NSW 2061, Australia,
in New Zealand by Random House New Zealand Ltd,
18 Poland Road, Glenfield, Auckland 10, New Zealand
and in South Africa by Random House (Pty) Ltd,
Endulini, 5a Jubilee Road, Parktown 2193, South Africa.

Printed and bound in Great Britain by
Clays Ltd, St Ives plc.

For Tommy and Jean Catlow, my parents,
and source of my love of food and in particular my sweet teeth!

ACKNOWLEDGEMENTS

I never know where to begin, but logically with the closest, my great source of strength and of the humour in life, Gog. I would also like to thank Carol Smith, my agent, and indeed Sally Gaminara and everyone at Doubleday. It sounds soapy to say how much I appreciate them all, but I do. You only need to experience working with a less than helpful publishing house to be ever grateful to the unique establishment of Transworld, of which Doubleday is a part.

Lunches

Contents

Introduction

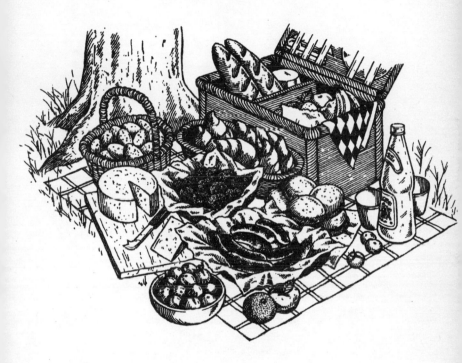

My life is one of contrasts, but they all complement each other. On the one hand I cook in our kitchen for our hotel guests. It is the happiest and most sociable of occupations, and Peter Macpherson, with whom I've now worked for 22 years, Claire Munro, Sharon MacInnes and I cook, chat, plan menus and have new ideas which prevent us from ever feeling stale about our work. This sociability contrasts with the solitude of writing, but the writing is fuelled by the continuous search for new ideas and new slants on dishes, many of which are in this book. We still cook very much influenced by the seasons, which I maintain is the right and proper way to appreciate food. Luckily I still feel that my greatest pleasure is feeding people – I love cooking, possibly even more than ever. I even love doing our cooking demonstrations, which involve a lot of work and preparation but once under way are invariably great fun – I think because of sharing with other people the common interest of a subject as absorbing as food! I do think, though, that there is more snobbery within the foodie world than in any other area of life. I see it as my personal mission to try and debunk as much of the carefully created mystique attached to food as is possible, and to try, through written recipes and cooking demonstrations, to make people realize that they can tackle various dishes they had previously thought beyond them – and this covers a vast range of items.

In this book there are suggestions for dishes intended for lunchtime eating but which are, of course, just as suitable for supper – with one or two exceptions. For instance, even I wouldn't eat a Steak, Kidney and Mushroom Pie or a Game Pudding in the evening. There is a chapter on food suitable for a business lunch – dishes which can be prepared ahead and eaten without too much fuss, to let those at the lunch concentrate on the matter in hand. A business lunch is the best way to hold a meeting. There is a chapter with suggestions for Sunday lunches – a very British institution, the Sunday lunch, and one which brings together friends and family members. Traditionally Sunday lunch consists of roast meats, but I have included a couple of alternatives which are more convenient for church-goers to pop in the oven than cooking a roast, with its accompanying gravy and so on. There are also vegetable dishes to accompany the recommended Sunday lunches.

There is a varied content to the chapter on picnics and food for eating outdoors. As a family we always have picnics in the winter as well as in the summer, and although these usually involve making a bonfire on a wild and deserted beach somewhere on Skye and cooking sausages and marshmallows, we always take a hot dish with us to sustain us. There is a chapter of ideas for lunches suitable for children, but in my opinion children should be and can be and are, for the most part, willing to eat just about everything an adult eats. The trouble with most children's attitude to food is their parents . . .! There is a chapter on brunches, a form of eating normally reserved for weekends. This covers a wide range of delicious eating, and brunch is a meal which can last most of the morning – my ideal way of entertaining.

The chapter containing pudding recipes is, for me, a sort of self-indulgence. It lets me do the sort of research I love, like making Dark Chocolate Soufflés several times to be quite sure I get them right! And then when we are all sick of eating Dark Chocolate Soufflés I move on to perfect Lemon and Vanilla Soufflés – but this chapter also contains more homely types of pudding recipes, like steamed Lemon and Syrup Sponge, and rich malt Bread and Butter Pudding.

There is a chapter on informal lunches, and a small chapter on lunches for special occasions, with some first course ideas. Some of the recipes in the business lunches chapter are also suitable for first courses, such as the Steamed Asparagus Salad with Lemon Aïoli, and the Watercress and Lime Mousse with Creamy Red Pepper Sauce.

Every chapter contains recipes which do not have meat among their ingredients. In line with very many other families in Britain today we eat far less meat than we used to, and this is reflected in the recipe content of this book. That said, we love meat when we do eat it, and we probably appreciate good meat the more for eating it less often.

I hope that the contents of this book will whet the appetites of those who read it, and also provide a spot of inspiration when it is needed, helping people to plan a lunch for any occasion when they are stuck for something to cook. Above all, I hope they enjoy the results!

Business Lunches

Savoury Profiteroles with (a) Beef and Horseradish, (b) Smoked Eel,

Cucumber and Crème Fraîche Fillings

Grilled Fish, Chops, or Chicken, with Savoury Butter

Mushroom and Broccoli Florentine

Brie, Lettuce and Bacon Toast Sandwiches with Mayonnaise

Watercress and Lime Mousse with Creamy Red Pepper Sauce

Tomato, Basil and Avocado Mousse

Goats' Cheese Roulade with Leek and Walnut Filling

Avocado and Salmon Terrine

Mushroom and Chicken Filo Parcels

Leek and Goats' Cheese Tart with Walnut Pastry

Chicken, Lemon and Herb Jellied Salad

Ham and Parsley Jellied Salad

Steamed Asparagus Salad with Saffron and Lemon (or Lime) Aïoli

BUSINESS LUNCHES

The contents of this chapter are not necessarily intended for those cooking for directors' lunches, although there are many recipes within this book which will hopefully cater for such occasions. These recipes are meant for those who both prepare and preside at a business lunch. Very often these days there is work to be done for whatever reason, school commitments, committees for a wide variety of purposes, and any meeting is much more fun when it can incorporate food as well – it makes the work much easier!

But having said that, there are a couple of points to bear in mind when planning food for such an occasion. I think it should be easy to eat, so as not to distract the participants from the subject under discussion – I don't serve intricate food which needs chiselling off bones, for example. Also I think that it is important to keep the smell potential to a minimum – the blue cheese, garlic and smoked mackerel based dishes don't really belong at a business lunch. Ideal food, for me, is one-dish food, like the Goats' Cheese Roulade with Leek and Walnut Filling, or the Watercress and Lime Mousse with Creamy Red Pepper Sauce (which also makes a very good first course, incidentally), both of which only need warm bread or rolls to accompany them.

In this chapter there are both hot weather and cold weather recipes – the Mushroom and Broccoli Florentine, or the Grilled Fish with Savoury Butter are ideal eating for a winter's day, whereas the Tomato, Basil and Avocado Mousse makes a perfect business lunch on a warm summer's day.

Savoury Profiteroles

These make a convenient and delicious business lunch. They can be prepared entirely in advance – the profiteroles can even be made and frozen, but I recommend that you put them in a solid box or container in case they get bashed in the freezer – it is easy to chip a frozen profiterole in a polythene bag. Also, if they have been frozen, they are much nicer if baked in a moderate oven for 7–10 minutes.

You can use a variety of fillings. I give you two idea
with rare roast beef, the other with smoked eel. You coul
smoked salmon or trout if you prefer, but smoked eel,
one of the best smoked fish, is now very widely availab
 These profiteroles need no further stodge in the form
accompany them, just a green salad and a tomato sal

SERVES 6

½ pt/285 ml water	*skinned and finely*
5 oz/140 g butter, cut into	*chopped (optional)*
bits	*A dash of Tabasco sa*
7 oz/200 g flour; remove 2	*3 oz/84 g grated Che*
tsp flour and add 2 tsp	*cheese*
mustard powder	*3 large eggs or 4 sm*
1 large clove of garlic,	*ones*

Rinse a baking tray with water. Put the ½ pt/285 ml wa
of butter into a saucepan over moderate heat and let the
in the water as it heats. Take care not to let the liquid
boil till the butter has melted completely. Meanwhil
flour and mustard twice into a bowl. Once the butter
let the liquid in the pan come to a rolling boil and add t
mustard all at once. Take the pan off the heat and beat
the dough rolls away from the sides of the pan — this
minute. Beat in the chopped garlic and the Tabasco
cheese, and then the eggs, one by one and beating
between each. You should end up with a glossy doug
 Now, by far the easiest method of getting even-sized pro
pipe them on to the damp baking tray, using a wide star-sh
Don't be put off at the thought of washing up the
afterwards, all you need do is slice off the choux mixtu
chuck it in the washing machine with your next very h
much easier and less messy than using two teaspoon
profiteroles on to the baking tray. Bake in a hot oven, 4
Gas Mark 7 for 10–15 minutes, then check them and slas

middle with a knife tip to release the steam that collects inside them. Bake for a further 10 minutes, or till they are quite firm to the touch. Use a palette knife to lift them from the baking tray on to a cooling rack.

Beef and Horseradish Filling

This is utterly delicious and simple.

1½ lb/675 g fillet steak	*A pinch of salt and plenty of*
2 tubs crème fraîche	*freshly ground black*
2 tsp creamy horseradish – the	*pepper*
best is made by Moniack	*1 tbsp snipped chives*

In a non-stick frying pan wiped out with olive oil, or on a char-grill, cook the meat over a high heat to the degree of rareness that you like. Let it cool, then, with a very sharp knife, trim away any bits of fat or gristle, and slice the meat into slivers.

Mix together the crème fraîche and the horseradish, salt, pepper and chives, and fold in the slivers of rare beef. Cut each profiterole in half and spoon in the filling.

Serve on a large plate surrounded by assorted salad greenery. I think that tomato salad (with plenty of torn-up basil leaves) makes a very good taste contrast, too.

Smoked Eel, Cucumber and Crème Fraîche Filling

The diced cucumber in this filling provides a good contrasting crunch.

---

1 cucumber	*2 tubs of crème fraîche*
1 lb/450 g smoked eel, sliced	*Plenty of freshly ground*
into slivers	*black pepper*

Peel the cucumber with a potato peeler (this takes seconds). Cut it into chunks, and then cut each chunk in half lengthways. Scoop out the seeds, and cut each piece into fine dice – without the seeds the diced cucumber won't seep liquid.

Mix together the slivers of eel, the diced cucumber, crème fraîche and pepper. Cut each profiterole in half and divide out the filling.

Serve on a large plate, surrounded by an assortment of lettuce leaves.

Grilled Fish, Chops, or Chicken with Savoury Butter

One of the simplest and quickest types of business lunch is straightforward grilled food. This can be varied widely – either fish, pieces of chicken (usually suprêmes, which are breasts of chicken, with skin on), or lamb chops. There are two points to bear in mind, though, with grilled food. One is that the grilling can toughen the fish, meat, or chicken if it is grilled under too fierce a heat. The other is that a plain grilled item needs to be dressed up, and one of the simplest ways to do this is also very convenient – serve a savoury butter with each piece of fish, meat, or chicken.

You can vary the flavours of these butters according to what you intend to serve them with. The Lime, Parsley and Chive Butter is good with all grilled fish and with grilled chicken, whereas the Red Pepper Butter is really only for serving with grilled chicken. Tomato and Basil Butter is delicious with grilled (or baked) salmon fillets or steak, and Chive and Mustard Butter is very good with lamb chops.

Choose a vegetable from the chapter on Sunday lunches to go with your grilled business lunch and for ease, and also because they are so good with the savoury butters, serve each of your guests a baked jacket potato.

Red Pepper Butter

This is especially good with grilled chicken or lamb chops, or with grilled or barbecued steaks.

2 red peppers	*Salt and freshly ground*
4 cloves of garlic, in their	*black pepper*
skins	*8 oz/225g slightly salted*
2 tbsp lemon juice	*butter*

Cut each pepper in half, scoop away the seeds and put the pepper halves skin side uppermost under a red-hot grill. Grill the peppers till their skin forms great black blisters, then take them out and put them in a polythene bag for 10 minutes. Then skin them and chop their flesh. Meanwhile, simmer the garlic cloves for 2 minutes, drain, cut off the ends of each clove and squeeze them from their skins – they should pop out easily – into a food processor. Add the chopped peppers and whiz, adding the lemon juice gradually. Season with salt and pepper.

In a bowl beat the softened butter with electric beaters, and gradually add the pepper and garlic purée, a small amount at a time, till the butter and purée are well combined. Wrap the butter in baking parchment, rolling it to an approximate log shape. Put this into the fridge, and when it is chilled, roll it firmly into a cylinder. Slice it thickly and put a slice or two on each piece of chicken or chop or steak.

Lime, Parsley and Chive Butter

This is good with any chicken, fish, or chops.

8 oz/225g slightly salted	*then dried on kitchen*
butter – I tend to use	*paper before grating*
Lurpak for everything	*finely*
Rind of 2 limes – the limes	*Juices of the limes*
well scrubbed under	*Salt and pepper*
running water to remove	*2 tbsp finely chopped*
the preservative with	*parsley and snipped*
which they are sprayed,	*chives mixed*

In a bowl beat the softened butter, easiest done using a hand-held electric whisk, and beat in the lime rinds and, drip by drip, the lime juice. Lastly, beat in the salt and pepper and the parsley and chives.

Form the butter into a log shape in baking parchment and put it into the fridge. When it is firm and chilled, roll it into a cylinder shape and wrap it in clingfilm. Slice it thickly, and serve one or two slices on top of the grilled food.

Tomato and Basil Butter

This is particularly good with grilled or baked salmon fillets or steaks.

8 oz/225g slightly salted butter	*2 tomatoes, each skinned, cut in half and their seeds scooped away, and the*
2 tsp tomato purée	
2 tbsp chopped basil	*tomato flesh cut into fine*
Salt and pepper	*dice*

I hate chopping basil with a knife, because metal tends to turn basil brown at the edges, but there is no alternative for this butter.

In a bowl beat the slightly softened butter, gradually adding the tomato purée and the chopped basil. Season with salt and pepper and mix in the diced tomatoes. Form the butter into a log shape wrapped in baking parchment. Put it into the fridge. When it is chilled and firm roll it into a neat cylinder shape, wrap it in clingfilm or baking parchment, and store it in the fridge. To serve, slice it thickly and put one or two slices on top of each piece of grilled fish.

Mustard and Chive Butter

This butter is especially good with grilled meats.

8 oz/225g slightly salted butter	*2 tsp Dijon mustard*
2 tsp mustard powder	*2 tbsp snipped chives*

In a bowl beat the slightly softened butter, gradually beating in the dry mustard and the Dijon mustard. Mix in the snipped chives, and scoop the butter on to a piece of baking parchment. Form it into an oblong and put it in the fridge. When it is chilled and firm, roll it into a neat cylinder shape and wrap it in clingfilm or baking parchment. Put it back in the fridge till you are ready to serve it. Slice it thickly, and put a slice on top of each grilled chop or steak.

Mushroom and Broccoli Florentine

Not at all consciously, all of us in our family tend to eat far fewer meals with meat as its main theme. This wholly vegetarian dish is an example, and it makes a perfect lunch for a working session. All you need to go with it is a basket of warm granary bread or rolls. If you can get good Lancashire cheese to make the sauce, do, but if not use a good strong Cheddar cheese.

SERVES 6

3 bags young spinach, weight 7 oz/200 g each bag	*2 oz/56 g butter and 3 tbsp olive or sunflower oil*
3 tbsp extra virgin olive oil	*1 lb/450 g mushrooms, wiped and chopped*
1 tbsp lemon juice	*2 cloves of garlic, skinned and finely chopped*
Salt, pepper, freshly grated nutmeg	*2 oz/56 g flour*
2 lb/900 g broccoli, cut into small florets using as much stem as possible	*1¼ pt/710 ml milk*
	5 oz/140 g grated cheese, Lancashire if possible

Put the bags of spinach into a microwave oven, if you have one, on a high setting for 2 minutes. Then tip the contents into a bowl and chop with a sharp knife, mixing in the olive oil and lemon juice, and some salt, pepper and nutmeg. If you don't have a microwave, put the spinach into a steamer with water, simmering until just before the spinach wilts – 3–4 minutes. Then put the broccoli florets into the steamer and steam till you can push a fork into the thickest bit of stem. Put the well chopped spinach into an ovenproof dish – a wide and fairly shallow one. Put the steamed broccoli over the spinach.

In a sauté pan melt the butter and heat the oil together and cook the chopped mushrooms till they almost squeak – by cooking them very well their flavour is greatly improved. Add the finely chopped garlic and cook for barely a minute before scattering in the flour. Stir it in well and cook for a further minute before adding the milk, gradually, and stirring continuously till the sauce reaches a simmering point. Simmer for a few moments then take the sauté pan off the heat, and stir in all but about a tablespoon of the grated cheese, and some more salt, pepper and nutmeg. Pour this sauce over the broccoli and spinach, and sprinkle the remainder of the grated cheese over the surface.

Before serving, put the dish under a hot grill, till the cheese on top melts and turns golden. This should be sufficient time for the contents to heat through. Keep it warm in a low temperature oven till you are ready to serve lunch.

Brie, Lettuce and Bacon Toast Sandwiches with Mayonnaise

These are not the sandwiches which are toasted when filled, but sandwiches made with toast instead of bread. The toast has to be made just before the sandwiches are to be eaten, but the fillings can be prepared well in advance, and toast sandwiches are utterly delicious. The most popular type are probably the classic bacon, lettuce and tomato, but this recipe is good, and you can put anything you choose inside the toast.

There are two ways to make sure that your toast sandwiches really are as good as they should be. One is to use good bread – my choice is for thick-sliced malted or granary bread. The other is to spread the hot toast with good mayonnaise instead of butter. In this case, mix a tablespoon of snipped chives into the mayonnaise before spreading the toast – it just adds more flavour to the other filling items.

ENOUGH FOR 4 TOAST SANDWICHES, GENEROUSLY FILLED

8 slices of thick granary bread
4 tbsp good mayonnaise – homemade if at all possible
1 tbsp snipped chives
Any lettuce leaves you choose – my preference is for rocket

1 lb/450 g Brie, rind left on and sliced as thinly as possible
8 rashers smoked streaky bacon, grilled till crisp, then broken up

Toast the bread. Spread each slice with the mayonnaise mixed with the snipped chives. Divide the lettuce leaves between four of the slices, then divide the slices of Brie and put them on top of the lettuce. Press the bits of bacon on to the other four mayonnaise-spread slices of toast, and put these on top of the other four. With a serrated knife cut each sandwich into quarters, slicing diagonally.

Watercress and Lime Mousse with Creamy Red Pepper Sauce

This is simple to make, can be done ahead of time, is easy and very good to eat, and makes a perfect dish for a business lunch. It also, made in individual ramekins, and the mousses turned out on to individual serving plates, makes an excellent first course. Watercress is a great favourite of mine, with its distinctive slightly peppery taste, and it is so good for us, being full of vitamin C.

SERVES 6 (8 as a first course)

1 pt/570 ml good chicken stock	*Salt, freshly ground black pepper, a dash of Tabasco*
1½ sachets of gelatine	*2 pots of crème fraîche*
2 bags (3 oz/75 g each) watercress, stalks and all	*(7 oz/200 g each)*
Juice of 1 lime and its finely grated rind	*2 egg whites*

Measure half the stock into a saucepan and warm gently. When the stock is hot – but not boiling – sprinkle in the gelatine and shake the pan carefully till the gelatine dissolves completely. Put the watercress into a processor with the rest of the stock and whiz till pulverized. Mix together the watercress liquid with the gelatine liquid, and stir in the grated lime rind and juice and seasonings.

Leave till it is beginning to gel – you can hurry this by putting the bowl into a washing-up bowl containing water and ice cubes, and stirring the contents of the watercress bowl to prevent a solid jelly forming in the base. It gels quite quickly, especially if it is in a metal bowl. Then take the watercress bowl out of the ice cubes and fold the crème fraîche into the watercress jelly.

In a separate bowl, whisk the egg whites till very stiff, and, using a large metal spoon, fold them quickly and thoroughly through the watercress. Pour into a glass or china serving bowl, or divide between 8 lightly oiled ramekins if you want to turn out the mousses. Cover with clingfilm and keep in the fridge till you are ready to eat.

Creamy Red Pepper Sauce

4 red peppers, or 3 if they are large	*2 tsp Balsamic vinegar*
½ pt/285 ml extra virgin olive oil	*Salt and freshly ground black pepper*

Cut each pepper in half and scoop out the seeds. Put them skin side uppermost on a baking tray under a hot grill. When great charred blisters have formed on the pepper skins, take them out from under the grill and put them in a polythene bag, or wrap them in clingfilm, and leave for 10–15 minutes. Then unwrap them and their skins should peel off easily. Cut them up roughly, put them into a food processor and whiz, adding the oil literally drop by drop – as for making mayonnaise. Lastly, add the Balsamic vinegar and the salt and pepper. Scrape this sauce from the processor into a bowl and store in the fridge, with the bowl covered, till you are ready to serve it with the Watercress and Lime Mousse.

If you are serving individual mousses made in ramekins and turned out, spoon some of the sauce over half of each turned-out mousse. Quite apart from the tastes going together very well, the colour contrast is very attractive.

Tomato, Basil and Avocado Mousse

This is such a good dish for light lunch on a summer's day. It can be made the evening before, and it looks good served with a mixed green salad and warm bread or rolls – for my taste, granary bread.

SERVES 6

½ pt/285 ml good chicken stock

1½ sachets (¾ oz/21 g) gelatine, or 6 leaves of gelatine

8 tomatoes, skinned, deseeded and whizzed to a purée – this should yield ¾ pt/420 ml

2 tbsp snipped chives

About 2 tbsp chopped basil leaves

6 tbsp good mayonnaise – a good bought one if not homemade

Salt and lots of freshly ground black pepper

2 egg whites

3 avocados, skinned, and the flesh chopped into neat dice and tossed in 3 tbsp lemon juice

Heat the stock and sprinkle the powdered gelatine into it – or feed in the leaves of gelatine. Shake the pan gently till the gelatine dissolves completely. Set the pan on one side till the contents cool. Then stir the cooled stock and gelatine into the tomato purée, along with the snipped chives and chopped basil. When the mixture begins to gel fold in the mayonnaise. Taste, and season with salt and pepper.

Whisk the egg whites till stiff and, with a large metal spoon fold them quickly and thoroughly through the tomato mousse. Spoon half the mousse into a serving dish or bowl. Cover with the diced avocado, then cover with the rest of the tomato mousse. Cover the bowl with clingfilm and leave to set.

If you like, garnish before serving with diced skinned and deseeded tomatoes tossed in a tablespoon of good olive oil, with more chopped basil. Scatter this around the edge of the mousse in its bowl.

Goats' Cheese Roulade with Leek and Walnut Filling

A cold roulade, which can be made the day before and assembled on the morning of the business lunch, is both delicious and easy to eat with a fork. Goats' cheese, leeks and walnuts are tastes which are made to be combined – they complement each other so well.

SERVES 6–8

1 pt/570 ml milk	*A stick of celery*
1 onion, cut in half	*A few peppercorns*
1 bayleaf	*About ½ tsp rock salt*
For the roulade:	*The strained flavoured milk*
2 oz/56 g butter	*2 oz/56 g grated Cheddar*
2 oz/56 g flour	*Extra pepper, if liked*
6 oz/170 g soft goats' cheese	*5 large eggs*

For the filling:
2 tbsp sunflower oil
6 medium leeks, washed,
   trimmed and sliced thinly
7 oz/200 g crème fraîche

3 oz/84 g walnuts (or pecans
   – even nicer), crushed and
   dry-toasted in a saucepan
   over heat for several
   minutes, shake the pan
A pinch of salt, freshly
   ground black pepper

Put the milk, onion, bayleaf, celery, peppercorns and rock salt into a saucepan over heat till a skin forms on the surface. Take the pan off the heat and leave to cool completely. The milk will be infused with all the flavours when it has cooled. Strain it when it is quite cold.

Line a baking tray with baking parchment, putting a dab of butter at each corner to hold the paper firmly in place. Melt the butter in a saucepan and stir in the flour. Let this cook for a minute before gradually adding the strained milk, stirring all the time – I find it best to use a wire whisk – until the sauce boils. Let it simmer gently for a moment, then take the pan off the heat and stir in the grated Cheddar cheese and the goats' cheese. Season with pepper if you think it needs more, and with nutmeg. Beat in the egg yolks, one by one.

Lastly, in a clean bowl whisk the egg whites till they are very stiff, and, with a large metal spoon, fold them quickly and thoroughly through the sauce. Pour and scrape this into the paper-lined tin and bake in a moderate oven, 350°F/180°C/Gas Mark 4, for 20–25 minutes, till the roulade feels firm to the touch and the surface is puffed up and golden. Take it out of the oven and cover with a slightly dampened teatowel. Leave to cool.

For the filling, measure the oil into a non-stick (if possible) frying or sauté pan and cook the sliced leeks over a moderate heat, stirring, till they are very soft when you stick a fork into a bit. Do try and slice them thinly, because not only do they look and eat better, but they take a very short time to cook – about 4–5 minutes. Let the leeks cool.

Lay a sheet of baking parchment on a work surface or table.

Scatter the chopped parsley over it. Take the short ends of paper in either hand and flip the roulade face down, as it were, on to the parsley. Peel the paper off the back of the roulade. Spread the crème fraîche over the surface, then scatter on the cooled nuts. Distribute the leeks over everything. I find a fork the easiest thing to use to do this. Season with a merest pinch of salt and with plenty of freshly ground black pepper.

Roll the roulade up away from you and slip it onto a serving plate. Leave it rolled up in its paper if you do this much more than an hour in advance, and then you can keep it a good rolled shape. Slip it off the paper before serving.

Avocado and Salmon Terrine

I like to make this in a Pyrex terrine-shaped dish. Even though I line the dish with clingfilm, I find that if I make it in a metal loaf or terrine tin lined with clingfilm the avocado turns brown in a much more marked fashion than it does with the clingfilm and the Pyrex. As I bought my Pyrex terrines in the hardware shop in Kyle of Lochalsh, I'm quite sure they would be easily obtainable in other places! This smooth avocado mixture has a layer of flaked salmon in the middle. It is quite a filling terrine, and needs only a green or mixed salad and warm bread to go with it.

SERVES 6–8

½ pt/285 ml good chicken stock and ¼ pt/140 ml dry white wine
1½ sachets of gelatine, or 6 leaves
1 lb/450 g salmon, poached, skinned, bones removed and flaked

½ tsp salt
1 tbsp finely chopped parsley and 1 tbsp snipped chives
4 avocados of the dark knobbly sort – I think these have the best taste, but if you use the larger

smooth-skinned type, 3	*2 tbsp Worcestershire sauce,*
avocados	*salt and pepper*
1 clove of garlic, skinned	*½ pt/285 ml crème fraîche*
and finely chopped	*Salt and pepper to season*
A dash of Tabasco sauce	

Line a 2½-pt/1.5 l Pyrex terrine (11 inches/28 cm long) with clingfilm, carefully pushing it into the corners of the dish as neatly as you can.

In a saucepan warm together the stock and wine. When they are hot but nowhere near boiling, sprinkle in the gelatine and shake the pan gently till it has dissolved completely. Pour a quarter of this liquid into the bowl containing the flaked salmon, and stir in the half teaspoon of salt, parsley and chives, mixing all together well. Scoop out the flesh from the avocados into a food processor. Add the chopped garlic, cooled gelatine, stock and wine, Tabasco and Worcestershire sauce and whiz all together till smooth. Add the crème fraîche whizzing it in briefly. Taste, and season with salt and pepper.

Scrape half this avocado mixture into the lined Pyrex terrine. With a fork, put the salmon and herbs mixture over the avocado mixture in the terrine, and scrape the remainder of the avocado mixture on top. Bang the terrine – carefully! – a couple of times on a work surface. Cover the dish with clingfilm and store in the fridge till you are ready to turn it out.

To turn out, dip the Pyrex dish in a basin of very hot water for two or three minutes, then turn it out on to a serving plate. Peel off the clingfilm at the very last minute before serving it, in thick slices.

Mushroom and Chicken Filo Parcels

A pile of these on a dish accompanied by a good salad makes a perfect lunch. You can prepare the parcels right up to the moment before you bake them, leave them covered with clingfilm on their baking tray in a cool place or a fridge, then just bake them before serving them hot. How many you allow per person does depend on the appetites of your working guests! This recipe makes 24 parcels.

SERVES 3–4

---

6 sheets of filo pastry
Melted butter – about 3 oz/
  84 g
For the filling:
2 tbsp sunflower or olive oil
  and 2 oz/56 g butter
1 lb/450 g mushrooms,
  wiped and chopped as
  finely as you can
2 cloves of garlic – be sure
  your guests like garlic
  and leave them out if they
  or you don't

8 oz/225 g reduced fat cream
  cheese, such as Lite, or
  Shape, or the full-fat
  Philadelphia cream
  cheese
1 lb/450 g cooked chicken
  breast, diced as small as
  you can, which will
  depend on how sharp
  your knife is
4 rashers of smoked streaky
  bacon, grilled till crisp
  then crumbled

Heat the oil and melt the butter together in a frying or sauté pan. When it is very hot add the chopped mushrooms, and cook them till they are almost crisp. Peel the garlic and chop it very finely and stir that, too, in amongst the mushrooms. Take the cooked mushrooms off the heat and cool them. In a quite large bowl beat the cream cheese till soft, and mix in the diced chicken, cooled mushrooms and garlic mixture, and the crumbled bacon.

Lay a sheet of filo on a table and brush it carefully all over with melted butter. Cover it as exactly as you can with a second sheet of filo and brush that, too, with melted butter. With a sharp knife cut the buttered filo in half, then cut each half in two strips, so you have four broad strips. Put a spoonful of filling in the bottom right corner of each strip. Fold into triangle shapes up to halfway up the strip, then cut across. Brush the triangle with melted butter and put it on a butter-brushed baking tray. Put a spoonful of filling in the bottom right hand corner of the halved strips and fold into triangles again. Brush the parcels with butter and put them on the baking tray. Repeat with the remaining sheets of filo.

Cover the baking tray with clingfilm and store the tray in the fridge till you are ready to bake the parcels. Put it into a hot oven, 425°F/220°C/Gas Mark 7, for 7–10 minutes, or till the filo is golden brown and crisp. Serve hot.

Leek and Goats' Cheese Tart with Walnut Pastry

The combined flavours of the walnuts, goats' cheese and leeks are delicious. This tart can be eaten either as a first course or as a main course. It is a most useful dish for those who don't eat meat.

SERVES 6–8

For the pastry:
3 oz/84 g walnuts
5 oz/140 g plain flour
4 oz/112 g butter, hard from the fridge, cut into bits
1 tsp icing sugar
Salt and pepper
For the filling:
2 tbsp olive oil
6 leeks, washed, trimmed and sliced thinly

2 goats' cheeses, crumbled after you have trimmed off the rinds
1/2 pt/285 ml single cream
2 large eggs + 2 egg yolks, beaten together
A good grinding of black pepper
A grating of nutmeg
A pinch of salt

Put all the ingredients for the pastry into a food processor and whiz till the mixture resembles fine crumbs. Pat these firmly around the sides and base of a flan dish approximately 9 inches/23 cm in diameter. Put the dish in the fridge for at least an hour, then bake in a moderate oven 350°F/180°C/Gas Mark 4, for 20–25 minutes, or till the pastry is golden. If the pastry looks as if it is slipping a bit down the sides of the flan dish as it cooks, press it up again with the back of a metal spoon.

To make the filling, heat the oil in a sauté pan and sauté the leeks till they are soft. With a slotted spoon, scoop them over the cooked pastry. Distribute the crumbled cheeses evenly over the leeks. Beat the cream into the eggs and yolks, and season with pepper, nutmeg and a tiny pinch of salt. Bake in a moderate oven, 350°F/180°C/Gas Mark 4, till just set, about 15–20 minutes. Serve warm.

Chicken, Lemon and Herb Jellied Salad

SERVES 6

1 chicken, free range if possible	*1 stick of lemon grass, crushed (optional)*
1 onion, cut in half	*2 egg whites*
Pared rind of 1 lemon	*1½ sachets, or ¾ oz/21 g, or 6 leaves of gelatine*
1 leek	
2 sticks of celery	*Juice of half a lemon*
Salt, peppercorns and a bayleaf	*2 tbsp chopped parsley*
	2 tbsp snipped chives
A piece of fresh ginger root, peeled (optional)	*Salt and pepper*

Put the chicken into a large saucepan with the onion, lemon rind, leek, celery, salt, peppercorns and bayleaf, and the ginger and/or lemon grass, and cover with water. Simmer, with the pan covered, for 1 hour. Test to see if the chicken is cooked by sticking the point of a knife into its thigh. If you are in any doubt, cook it for a further 10–15 minutes.

Leave the chicken in the stock till it is cool, then take it out, cut all the flesh from the bones, and weigh out 1 lb/450 g. Cut this into pieces as neatly as possible. Keep the remaining chicken for a salad or a fricassee.

Put the carcase back in the stock and simmer gently, with the lid on the pan, for 2–3 hours (*or overnight in an Aga or Rayburn oven*).

Strain 1½ pt/850 ml of the stock into a pan and put it on a moderate heat. Whisk the egg whites till frothy, then whisk them into the stock in the pan and continue to whisk till the stock simmers. Then draw the pan off the heat and leave it to cool. This helps to clarify the stock. If you like, add the egg shells as well as the lightly whisked whites. Skim off the whites and strain the stock.

Reheat ¼ pt/140 ml of the stock – do not let it boil – and dissolve the gelatine in it. Stir this liquid into the rest of the stock and add the lemon juice. Leave this mixture till it is just beginning to jell, then stir in the herbs, salt and pepper to taste, and the chicken.

Pour everything into a ring mould 9 inches/23 cm in diameter and put it into the fridge to set. This freezes well. Unmould before serving.

Ham and Parsley Jellied Salad

I always think that parsley is a greatly underrated herb, too often used only as garnish. I love all parsley, but flat-leaved parsley has by far the best flavour. Combined with the ham in this recipe it makes a very favourite lunch, whether as a business lunch or not! But its benefits for a business lunch are that it has to be made a day in advance to let the jelly set, and it is easy both to serve and to eat with a fork, therefore leaving one hand free for writing whenever necessary. It is good served with a tomato and basil salad and a green salad, and, if you like – I always do like – warm bread.

Serves 4–6

1½ lb/675 g ham, trimmed
of gristle and excess fat
before weighing, then cut
into cubes about ½ inch/1
cm thick – the better the
ham, either roast or
boiled, the better this
salad will be

3 good tbsp chopped
parsley, preferably the
flat-leaved type

1 pt/570 ml good vegetable
or ham stock, either
freshly made or made
using a cube containing
no additives – these are
made by either Kallo or
Friggs

2 sachets of gelatine

½ pt/285 ml dry white wine
– if you prefer to leave
out the wine just use an
extra ½ pt/285 ml of
stock

Plenty of freshly ground
black pepper

Salt if you think it
necessary, but taste first –
need or not will depend
on how salty your ham is

Mix together the cubed ham and the chopped parsley. In a small saucepan heat ½ pt/285 ml of the stock and sprinkle in the gelatine, shaking the pan gently till it dissolves completely. Then stir this into the rest of the stock and wine. Season with pepper, and salt if needed.

Put the ham and parsley into a 2½ pt/1.5 l ring mould, or a loaf or terrine tin, and carefully pour in the stock and gelatine. As it sets, fork it through once or twice to keep the ham and parsley evenly distributed through the setting jelly. When set, unmould and surround with lettuce.

Steamed Asparagus Salad with Saffron and Lemon (or Lime) Aïoli

I think there is something luxurious about a pile of asparagus, and it makes a perfect lunch – nothing could be simpler. The asparagus can be steamed earlier in the morning. The saffron and lemon (or lime if you like) aïoli can be made a couple of days in advance, and all you need to do before your business lunch party arrives is arrange the asparagus on a large serving plate and surround it with assorted lettuce leaves. But I do think that sieved hardboiled eggs mixed with snipped chives make a very good garnish – the tastes all go together so well, and it looks good, too.

For a main course allow a generous amount of asparagus per person, about ½ lb/225 g. Steam the asparagus till the thickest stalk is just tender when you push the fork into it. Immediately take the asparagus off the heat and run cold water briefly through it, to refresh the colour. Let it drain, and pat it gently with kitchen paper to absorb excess moisture.

For the garnish, hardboil 3 eggs (for 6 people), shell them, and chop them roughly. Put them into a sieve and push them through – the back of a ladle is best for this. Mix them, using a fork, with 2 tbsp snipped chives, and scatter this over the steamed asparagus in its serving dish with lettuce around.

Saffron and Lemon (or Lime) Aïoli

ENOUGH FOR 6 SERVINGS

1 whole egg + 1 egg yolk	¼ pt/140 ml each of olive
1 tsp French mustard	and sunflower oils, mixed
½ tsp salt and a good	1 tbsp lemon juice, and the
grinding of black pepper	grated rind of 1 lemon
½ tsp sugar	2 generous pinches of
2 cloves of garlic, poached for	saffron, soaked in 1 tbsp
1 minute, then skinned	wine vinegar

Put the egg, yolk, mustard, salt and pepper, sugar and poached garlic into a food processor and whiz, adding the oils drop by drop till you have a thick mayonnaise, then adding them in a steady trickle. In a small pan gently warm the vinegar and the lemon juice and rind with the saffron – the colour will seep from the strands of saffron. Cool this, and whiz it into the mayonnaise. Serve in a bowl to accompany the asparagus salad.

Brunch

Smoked Haddock with Scrambled Eggs

Cold Baked Ham

Lemon and Raisin Cinnamon Pancakes

Muffins with Blueberries

Apple Pancakes with Crisp Bacon, Black Pudding and Maple Syrup

Crème Fraîche Coffee Cake

Kedgeree

Hot Fresh Fruit Salad with Honey, Ginger and Cardamom

Arranged Fruit Platter

Scrambled Eggs with Tomatoes and Red Peppers on Croûtons

Eggs Benedict

Potato Scones

Oatcakes

Omelettes with Rocket (or Baby Spinach) and Goats' Cheese

Grilled Tomatoes with Ginger and Basil

Pigs in Blankets

Sausagemeat Soufflé

Mushroom Brunch Soufflé

Devilled Kidneys

Homemade Muesli

Spicy Raisin Buns

Apple Spice Cake

Iced Coffee with Cinnamon

Creamy Mushrooms with Croûtons

Stuffed Croissants

BRUNCH

Brunch is a wonderful way to entertain. It is also an ideal occasion for a lazy, leisurely meal over almost half a day when all the family are at home and you want to prolong the sociability of an ordinary breakfast or lunch by combining the two. Brunch gives me the leeway to cook a variety of foods which wouldn't normally belong in the same meal, but which do go acceptably and perfectly together for a brunch. By this I mean that I can have fresh squeezed orange juice, with or without champagne or sparkling wine to transform it into Buck's Fizz, and I can also have an arrangement of summer fruits, or, in chilly weather, a Hot Fresh Fruit Salad, spiked with ginger and flavoured with the aromatic spice cardamom.

I can have a wide variety of main course dishes to choose from – Eggs Benedict, with poached eggs on halved buttered muffins and good ham, with hollandaise sauce over it all, or a good Kedgeree. Some readers may notice that the recipes for Kedgeree and Smoked Haddock with Scrambled Eggs have appeared in my previous book, *Suppers*, but how could I not include them in a chapter on Brunch?

Another favourite is scrambled eggs mixed with skinned chopped tomatoes and roast red peppers, served with large croûtons, which is a way of describing the best type of fried bread. (How I love fried bread, and how nearly everyone else loves fried bread too, whenever the subject is mentioned! But call it a croûton, and people will eat it without so much as a twinge of the awful guilt which prevents most people indulging in eating fried bread – the guilt lies in the word 'fried'.) Large croûtons (fried bread!) are to be found, again, as the accompaniment for the Creamy Mushrooms, which are an ideal brunch dish for non-meat eaters, but which are so good for those who do eat meat when accompanied by crisply grilled bacon. Bacon also makes a perfect accompaniment for the Apple Pancakes, which are made from a crêpe batter with grated apples folded into the mixture.

There are a number of sticky breads and coffee cakes which are delicious at a brunch. The Spicy Raisin Buns, or the Apple Spice Cake, or the Crème Fraîche Coffee Cake, are all easy to make and so good to eat. I have included an iced coffee recipe which is ideal for a hot summer brunch; it is flavoured with cinnamon, a very complementary spice with coffee.

Smoked Haddock with Scrambled Eggs

This is very convenient to make, because you can cook and flake the smoked haddock (you can use smoked cod instead, if you like) and beat up the eggs with Tabasco and milk the night before the brunch. All you need do then, just before eating, is melt the butter in the saucepan and cook the eggs, folding in the flaked smoked fish and the chopped parsley just before serving.

SERVES 6–8

1½ lb/675 g smoked haddock – undyed	A good dash of Tabasco sauce
Milk and water to cook the fish	Salt and black pepper
12 large eggs	3 oz/84 g butter
¼ pt/140 ml full fat milk	1–2 tbsp finely chopped parsley (optional)

Feel the fish, on a board, and cut out or pull out all bones. Put the fish into a saucepan and cover with milk and water. Put the pan on a moderate heat until a skin forms. Take the pan off the heat and let the fish cool in the milk. Then take it out (keep the milk, and use it for potato and onion soup), flake the fish and set it on one side. Beat together the eggs, milk, Tabasco, salt and pepper (go easy on the salt – a pinch will do, because the fish will add saltiness). Do this the night before the brunch.

Melt the butter in a heavy-based (preferably non-stick, for easier washing up) saucepan. Pour in the egg mixture and cook, stirring occasionally, till the scrambled eggs are softly firm. Stir in the flaked smoked fish. Dish up – the eggs will cease to cook once the cold fish is folded in, but take care not to cook them till they are too firm. If you like, stir in a couple of tablespoons of finely chopped parsley at the last moment before serving.

Cold Baked Ham

Good ham is invaluable as part of a brunch. It goes so well with just about everything savoury in this chapter, fishy dishes included. For example, the Smoked Haddock with Scrambled Eggs is good with cold sliced ham. Whether you get smoked or green ham is up to you, but it is much better to cook your own, because then you get a good ham stock to use for lentil soup at a later date.

Much as I prefer to buy and cook meat on the bone, it is undeniably easier to buy boned ham. Also, if ham is left on the bone, the part nearest the bone tends to get awfully dry after a few days.

SERVES 6–8 WITH SOME LEFT OVER, ALWAYS USEFUL

A piece of boned ham weighing about 5 lb/2.25 kg	*A few peppercorns*
	Whole cloves
2 onions, each cut in half	*4 tbsp thick honey*
2 sticks of celery, each broken in two	*3 tbsp good quality (i.e. not very vinegary) grainy mustard*
3 bayleaves	

Put the ham into a large saucepan with the onions, celery, bayleaves and peppercorns and cover it all with water. Bring it to simmering point, then cover the pan with a lid and simmer very gently for 20 minutes to the pound less 30 minutes. Let the ham cool in the stock.

When it is cold, take it out of the stock, cut off the skin, and then with a sharp knife cut diagonally across the fat going one way, then diagonally going in the other direction, and stick a clove in each diamond shape in the fat. Make a paste with the honey and mustard (dip the spoon in hot water between each spoonful when measuring out the honey so that it slips off more easily) and spread it over the ham. Roast in a hot oven, 425°F/220°C/Gas Mark 7, for 35–40 minutes, basting it several times as the honey and mustard mixture will slip off the ham. Watch out that it doesn't burn. Put about 4 tablespoons of water into the roasting tin with the ham, to make the washing up easier.

When the ham is cooked, take it out of the tin, put it on a serving plate and leave it to cool. Cover it when cold. Slice it thinly to serve at the brunch.

Lemon and Raisin Cinnamon Pancakes

A pancake in Scotland is a drop scone south of the border. These are of the drop scone variety as opposed to being crêpes.

MAKES 8 PANCAKES

4 oz/112 g plain flour	*Grated rind of 1 lemon*
1½ tsp baking powder	*1 oz/28 g butter, melted*
2 tsp cinnamon	*2 oz/56 g raisins*
1 egg mixed well with ¼ pt/	
140 ml milk	

Sieve together the flour, baking powder and cinnamon into a bowl. With a flat or small balloon whisk gradually mix in the egg and milk mixture, the grated lemon rind and the melted butter and the raisins. Mix really well. Cover the bowl with a cloth and leave for 30 minutes.

Heat a griddle, or a large non-stick frying or sauté pan. Wipe it out with a small amount of butter. Drop spoonfuls of the pancake mixture on to the hot surface. When they form small bubbles, turn them over, using a palette knife. They will puff up very slightly. Lift them off on to a cooling rack and cover with a cloth till you are ready to serve them, with butter.

This makes eight, but you could make smaller pancakes and have twelve.

Muffins with Blueberries

You can put all types of fruit into muffins, but for me the best by far are those made with blueberries. It is now so easy to buy blueberries in Britain. It is tempting, I know, to buy those packet mixes which have small tins of blueberries in the packet, but wait till you open the tin of blueberries – minuscule berries the size of a pinhead, and with about as much flavour. There is no substitute for making your own fruit muffins.

MAKES 12–15

12 oz/340 g plain flour	*¼ teaspoon salt*
4 oz/112 g sugar – I use soft	*1 large egg, mixed well with*
brown, but you can use	*¼ pt/140 ml milk and*
caster	*2 oz/56 g melted butter*
2 tsp baking powder	*4 oz/112 g blueberries*

Sieve the dry ingredients together. Beat in the egg, milk and butter. Fold in the blueberries. Put paper cases into muffin or Yorkshire pudding tins and divide the blueberry mixture between them. Bake for 30–40 minutes in a moderate oven, 350°F/180°C/ Gas Mark 4.

Apple Pancakes with Crisp Bacon, Black Pudding and Maple Syrup

These pancakes are delicious made to eat with crisp bacon and slices of grilled (or baked) black pudding. Serve them with butter and maple syrup. It is so much easier to buy real maple syrup in Britain these days, instead of the thick, sickly syrup with an artificial maple taste which was all we used to be able to find.

MAKES ABOUT 16

8 oz/225 g plain flour
A pinch of salt
2½ tsp baking powder
1 oz/28 g caster sugar (or soft brown sugar)
2 eggs, beaten with just less than ½ pt/285 ml milk

2 oz/56 g butter, melted
2 good eating apples, skin peeled off (I use a potato peeler), and the apples grated and mixed with 2 tsp lemon juice (which helps prevent discoloration)

Sieve the dry ingredients and mix in the eggs, milk and butter. Mix well, then mix in the grated apples. Cover the bowl with a cloth and leave for 30 minutes. Then make up the pancakes by heating a griddle, or a large non-stick frying or sauté pan. Rub it around with butter, sparingly. Drop spoonfuls of the apple mixture into the hot pan, fairly spaced out. When tiny bubbles start appearing on the surface, turn them over with a palette knife. Cook for about half a minute on the other side, then lift them on to a cooling rack, and cover them with a cloth till you are ready to serve them, with butter, maple syrup, crisp bacon and black pudding.

Crème Fraîche Coffee Cake

The gooey type of coffee cake, to be eaten with coffee rather than made from it, found so readily in America is my idea of heaven. I once shared a coffee cake for six with one great friend whilst Godfrey and I were on holiday with her in Florida. And then I wonder why the buttons on my skirts need to be let out . . . but this is perfect brunch food, and we don't eat brunch every day.

MAKES 12–16 SQUARES

3 oz/84 g chopped pecan nuts (or walnuts, if you can't get pecans)	*together till thick and pale*
1 tbsp cinnamon	*12 oz/340 g plain flour*
2 oz/56 g demerara sugar	*1 tsp baking powder*
4 oz/112 g butter	*½ tsp bicarbonate of soda*
8 oz/225 g caster sugar	*½ pt/285 ml crème fraîche (or soured cream)*
2 large eggs, whisked	*2 tsp vanilla essence, or a few drops vanilla extract*

Butter a 9-inch/23-cm square cake tin and line the base with baking parchment.

Mix together the chopped nuts, cinnamon and demerara sugar. Beat together the butter and caster sugar till they are light and fluffy. Add the eggs, alternately with the flour, baking powder and bicarbonate of soda, sieved together. Lastly beat in the crème fraîche (or soured cream) and vanilla essence. Put this batter into the prepared cake tin. Sprinkle the cinnamon and nuts mixture over the surface.

Bake in a moderate oven, 350°F/180°C/Gas Mark 4, for 35 minutes, or till when you stick a knife into the middle of the cake it comes out clean. Serve this cake warm, cut into squares.

Kedgeree

If you leave out the chopped hardboiled eggs, this will freeze beautifully.

1½ lb/675 g smoked haddock or smoked cod	*12 oz/340 g long-grain rice – I use Basmati rice*
Milk and water to cover the fish in a saucepan	*freshly ground black pepper*
1 onion, cut in half	*2 oz/56 g raisins (optional, but delicious)*
2 oz/56 g butter	*6 hardboiled eggs, chopped*
1 onion, finely chopped	*2 tbsp finely chopped parsley*
1 tsp medium strength curry powder	

Put the fish into a saucepan and cover with milk and water, and add the halved onion. Cover with a lid, and over a moderate heat bring the liquid to barely simmering point. Take the pan off the heat and leave to cool completely. Then strain the liquid into a jug or bowl, and carefully flake the fish, removing all bones and skin.

Melt the butter in a saucepan and add the chopped onion. Cook till the onion is transparent, then stir in the curry powder and the rice, and cook, stirring, for a couple of minutes so that every grain of rice is coated with butter. Then pour in the strained fish liquid. Simmer gently till the rice is cooked – it should absorb virtually all the liquid. Fork in the flaked fish and season with pepper. Fork in the raisins, if you are including them, and chopped hardboiled eggs, one per person.

Reheat gently, adding more bits of butter, and stir in the chopped parsley just before serving. If you want to freeze it, do so before you add the eggs and parsley.

Hot Fresh Fruit Salad with Honey, Ginger and Cardamom

This is one of the nicest ways to eat fruit at any time of the day, but it makes a delicious course for a winter brunch. If you don't like the

taste of honey – and it is surprising just how many people don't –
use maple syrup instead.

SERVES 6–8

Half a 1lb pot of thick honey
3 good eating apples, e.g.
  Cox's, peeled, cored and
  sliced
4 cardamom seeds, crushed,
  and the tiny black seeds
  removed
1 medium pineapple, skin
  cut off and the flesh cut
  into chunks

½ lb/225 g grapes, black or
  green, whichever is best,
  cut in half and pips
  removed
4–6 pieces of stem ginger,
  drained of their syrup
  and chopped
3 pink grapefruit, skin and
  pith cut off and the flesh
  cut into segments, cutting
  inside the pith.

Melt the honey in a wide sauté pan and gently cook the sliced
apples in it for a few minutes. Stir in the cardamom, pineapple,
grapes, ginger and grapefruit. Heat them all together gently – the
only possible casualty might be the grapefruit, which tend to break
up a bit in the heat. Keep the fruit salad warm till you are ready to
serve.

Arranged Fruit Platter

Rather than a fresh fruit salad as such, a large plate, or 'ashet' as
such a plate is called in Scotland (from the word *assiette* in French),
with sliced or whole fruit, depending on what they are, both looks
more attractive and gives you great fun artistically. It can also form
the centrepiece of the brunch table, or sideboard.

2 small, ripe melons, such as Gallia, each cut in half from the Arctic to the Antarctic, as it were, rather than round the	*Equator – slice each half, removing the seeds, into slices about 1 inch/2½ cm thick, and cut off the skin.*

Other fruits could be raspberries, strawberries (leave several with their stalks and leaves on, for decoration), blueberries, and skinned peaches or nectarines – you can leave these in halves, or slice them, or chop them and mix them with the raspberries.

Arrange the fruits in sections, rather than all jumbled together as with a fruit salad. Make a central focus to the plateful with, perhaps, a pile of strawberries, with those with their leaves and stalks on scattered around the rest of the plate.

Scrambled Eggs with Tomatoes and Red Peppers on Croûtons

These both look good and taste good. You can do so much of the preparation the night before – the eggs can be beaten all ready to scramble, the tomatoes can be skinned, de-seeded and chopped, and the peppers can be grilled, skinned and chopped, all ready to fold into the scrambled eggs. The croûtons (fried bread) can be made the day before, too, and reheated.

Butter and a small amount of olive oil for frying *Bread, crusts removed, cut into whatever size you*	*choose – I like to make the croûtons about 2 inches/5 cm square* *3 oz/84 g butter*

1 clove of garlic (optional),
   skinned and chopped
   finely
12 large eggs, beaten well
   with ¼ pt/140 ml creamy
   milk
Salt, pepper and a dash of
   Tabasco sauce
4 tomatoes, each skinned,
   de-seeded, and the flesh
   chopped neatly

3 red peppers, each cut in
   half and put, skin side
   uppermost, under a red-
   hot grill till their skins
   form black blisters, then
   put them into a polythene
   bag for 10 minutes, after
   which peel off the skins
   and chop the peppers

In a non-stick sauté or frying pan, melt the butter and heat the oil together. Fry the crustless croûtons till they are golden brown on either side. When they are cooked put them on to several thick-nesses of kitchen paper, to absorb excess grease. Alternatively, you can brush a baking tray with melted butter, brush the crustless bread with melted butter on both sides, and bake your croûtons – you actually use less butter and oil this way.

Melt the 3oz/84 g butter in a heavy-based saucepan. Add the garlic and cook for a minute, then add the egg mixture. Cook over a moderate (not high) heat, stirring till the eggs are just softly firm. Take care not to let them get too solid. Then take the pan off the heat, season with salt, pepper and Tabasco (if you haven't already mixed it into the egg mixture), and stir in the chopped tomatoes and peppers. The heat of the eggs should heat through the tomatoes and peppers.

Dish up into a hot shallow dish, with the hot croûtons around the edge of the eggs.

Eggs Benedict

I first ate this most delectable of all brunch food on a far too brief visit to New Orleans what seems – and is – an age ago, in 1967. As with everything you cook, the very best ingredients make the difference between an ordinary result and a superlative one. I like to use unsmoked roast (or boiled) ham, trimmed of all fat. There is no denying that Eggs Benedict is a last-minute concoction, and there just can't be short cuts. This makes it a special brunch for 3–4 people but it isn't practical to make it for many more, unless, that is, you have help in the making.

SERVES 2

---

4 large egg yolks
6 tbsp white wine vinegar,
 reduced by two-thirds in
 a small saucepan with a
 slice of onion, a bayleaf, a
 few peppercorns and a
 couple of crushed parsley
 stalks (to release their
 flavour)

8 oz/225 g butter, cut in bits
2 muffins, split and toasted
 at the last moment –
 toasted too soon, the
 muffins turn unpleasantly
 leathery in texture – and
 buttered
4 slices of the best ham
4 large eggs, poached

Whisk the egg yolks with a small balloon whisk, adding the strained, hot reduced vinegar. Put the bowl over a pan of just simmering water and beat in the butter, bit by bit, till all is incorporated and you have a thick and glossy hollandaise sauce.

Put two buttered toasted muffin halves on a warm serving plate for each person. Cover each with a slice of ham. Put a poached egg on top of each slice of ham, and divide the hollandaise sauce between the four eggs, spooning it over them. Eat as immediately as you can – it will keep warm for 5 minutes or so without deteriorating too much, but it is really nicest eaten at once.

Potato Scones

Potato scones are an essentially Scottish item, and they make such good breakfast eating, when accompanied by bacon, sausages, black pudding and mushrooms. But they are also awfully good just spread liberally with butter (which melts as it is spread) and Marmite, and eaten with grilled tomatoes. They are cooked on top, as it were, rather than baked – like cooking pancakes or drop-scones. How many you get out of this mixture does depend on the size you cut them.

MAKES ABOUT 8

1 lb/450 g potatoes, boiled till tender, then drained well, mashed well, and beaten with a wooden	*spoon, adding 2 oz/56 g butter* *Salt and pepper* *3 oz/84 g plain flour, sieved*

Season with salt and pepper and beat in the flour. On a floured surface roll out the potato dough and cut into triangles or circles. Lightly oil or butter a griddle or a non-stick frying or sauté pan, and when it is hot, slip the scones on and cook them for about 1½ minutes each side, if they are very thin – for longer if they are thicker. Once cooked, put them on to a wire rack and cover them with a cloth till you are ready to serve them. Serve warm.

Oatcakes

In the previous recipe for potato scones I mentioned that they are a Scottish item, but nothing could be more Scottish (except porridge) than oatcakes. But how oatcakes are made, their thickness and even their shape, varies from region to region. Far and away the best oatcakes to buy are all made in Orkney, and you can buy thick and thin versions – I can never make up my mind which I like best. This is how I make oatcakes, as taught by Annette Stephens several years ago when she lived and worked with us – happy days! She is now Annette Rennie. You can store them in an airtight container for several days.

8 oz/225 g coarse oatmeal –	*8 oz/225 g wholemeal flour*
I like to take out 2 tbsp	*½ tsp salt*
and substitute 2 tbsp	*4 oz/112 g lard – it should*
pinhead oatmeal, which I	*be bacon fat, but there is*
love	*never enough*
	4 oz/112 g butter

Mix together the oatmeal, flour and salt. Rub in the lard and butter. I use the fats straight from the fridge and cut them into the dry ingredients with a knife. When they are cut and mixed as finely as possible, mix all to a stiff dough with a little cold water. Dust a surface with oatmeal and roll out the dough. Cut into oblongs, squares, triangles, or circles – whichever you prefer. Slip them on to a baking tray and bake in a fairly hot oven, 400°F/200°C/Gas Mark 6, for 10–15 minutes, or until set and lightly browned. Cool them on a wire rack.

Omelettes with Rocket (or Baby Spinach) and Goats' Cheese

I reckon on making omelettes for a brunch only for a few people; to try to turn out omelettes for much more than four would obliterate you, the cook, from the sociable side of the brunch altogether. I was once at a large party where omelettes were the main part of the brunch (it was in New York city) but there were five chefs cooking them, and each had an array of bowls containing different fillings from which the guests chose, for their individual orders! I have never forgotten it.

This recipe makes omelettes for four – keep the first one for your own, as it will have to sit and keep warm the longest.

8 large eggs	*8 oz/225 g soft goats' cheese,*
4 tbsp water	*broken into quite small*
A good dash of Tabasco	*bits*
sauce	*3 oz/84 g rocket (or baby*
Salt and pepper	*spinach), torn into small*
Butter for the omelette pan	*bits (or chopped)*

If you have a large omelette pan you can make two large omelettes (4 eggs each, and cut each one in half, although individual omelettes do look better). Beat together well the eggs, water, Tabasco, salt and pepper. Heat the crêpe or omelette pan (mine is one and the same pan) with a dab of butter in it. When the butter is foaming pour in about a quarter of the mixture – this is easiest if you mix it up in one of those very large measuring jugs which have a 4-pint/2½-litre capacity and which can so well double up as mixing bowls. Lakeland Plastics sell them, but so do a wide variety of other outlets, too, these days.

Cook the mixture briefly in the omelette pan, lifting up the edges to let the runny mixture slip underneath the firm top. When it is mostly firm, scatter a quarter of the broken-up goats' cheese on top, and a quarter of the torn-up rocket (or spinach). Cook for about half a minute longer, then fold over and slip on to a warmed plate. Repeat, till you have made three more omelettes.

These are good served with the Grilled Tomatoes in the next recipe.

Grilled Tomatoes with Ginger and Basil

These can be put ready the night before, all ready to pop under the grill, or to bake in the oven.

8 tomatoes, washed well	*Powdered ginger*
Salt and pepper	*Basil leaves*
A pinch of sugar	*Butter*

Cut the tomatoes in half and season each half with salt, pepper and a tiny pinch of sugar. Sieve a small amount of ginger over each, and scatter torn-up basil leaves on top. Lastly, dot each tomato half with butter.

Grill or bake till the tomatoes are soft. These keep warm very well without spoiling.

Pigs in Blankets

I first ate these in Georgia, when Godfrey and I were staying in the small village of Culloden, for the Culloden Highland Games. We were lucky enough to stay in an old hotel, which had been in the same family for over a hundred years. Culloden is just a few miles from Juliette, the small village where *Fried Green Tomatoes at the Whistlestop Café* was filmed, and the whole area is enchanting. The earth is a vivid red, there are so many people of Scots ancestry, indeed the county in which Culloden is situated is called Monroe County, and the Games were the best we have ever been lucky enough to attend. The whole atmosphere is one of warmth and friendly informality. And because the Holmes Hotel was small, with a veranda running around the front and one side of the house, we stayed there amongst other very good Macdonald friends – it was really like staying in a very nice house, and we became good friends with our host and hostess, Jimmy and Clarene Wilson.

For breakfast each day we ate delicious and interesting food, all different to us. Pigs in Blankets were among our favourites! They are so simple, but so good, and they are so suitable for any brunch. They consist of small sausages, usually frankfurters (and when I make them at home I always use frankfurters), wrapped in a scone mixture. I was told that the small pigs could have pastry blankets instead of scone-type blankets, but I think the scone mixture is best. They are served with tart jelly – this could be blackcurrant jelly, or even rowan jelly, providing it is made with sweet apples and spiced with a stick of cinnamon.

Be sure to make enough pigs, because they really are very popular, but do watch out not to make the blankets too thick! The first time I made them I made this mistake, and the pigs were fine but their blankets were rather stodgy. They must be thinly rolled out.

MAKES 20

12 oz/340 g self-raising flour	*1 tbsp sunflower oil*
½ tsp salt	*Just less than ½ pt/285 ml*
1 tsp baking powder	*milk*
1 egg	*10 Frankfurters, cut in half*

Sieve the dry ingredients together into a bowl. Beat together the egg, oil and milk in a mixing bowl. Stir it into the flour mixture, adding a bit more sieved flour if the dough is too sticky. Roll out thinly on a floured surface, into a rectangular shape. Cut into triangles to hold a half frankfurter each, wrapped so the frank is facing opposite corners and the blanket folds point to the middle around the sausage. Put them on to baking trays and bake in a hot oven, 425°F/220°C/Gas Mark 7, for about 10 minutes. The scone mixture blanket will be puffed up and pale golden. Serve them warm, with a sharp fruit jelly to eat with them.

Sausagemeat Soufflé

This isn't a soufflé in the real sense, but it is another breakfast dish we enjoyed whilst in Georgia, and one I have made several times since then. It comes in many versions – some have chopped peppers in them – but this is how I make this very good dish. It does make a difference if you use really good sausages: the Lincoln pork sausages from Marks & Spencer, or their free-range sausages, or their butcher-style sausages, are all perfect to use. You can prepare the whole dish, cover it with clingfilm and leave it in the fridge overnight, only needing the clingfilm removed before you pop it in the oven. It takes a good 45 minutes to cook.

SERVES 6–8

2 tbsp sunflower oil	*Baked brown bread, (you*
1½ lb/675 g best quality	*can use white if you*
pork sausages, each slit	*prefer), crusts removed*
with a sharp knife and	*and the bread cut into*
the skins removed	*1-inch/2.5-cm cubes – you*
3 tsp made-up mustard,	*will need 6 slices*
either English or French	*8 large eggs, beaten with*
A good dash of Tabasco	*1 pt/570 ml milk*
sauce	*Salt and pepper*
3 tsp tomato purée	*4 oz/112 g grated cheese*

Heat the oil in a heavy sauté pan and cook the skinned sausage-meat, breaking up the sausage shape with your wooden spoon. Cook till the meat looks as if it is beginning to brown. Stir in the mustard, Tabasco and tomato purée.

Lightly oil a 4–5 pint/2.5–3 litre ovenproof dish and put the cubes of bread in the bottom. Scatter the cooked sausagemeat over the bread (avoiding any of the grease from the sauté pan). Season the egg and milk mixture, pour this over the sausagemeat and bread, and scatter the grated cheese into the mixture. Cover, and leave in the fridge overnight.

Bake in a moderate oven, 350°F/180°C/Gas Mark 4, for 45–50 minutes. It should be firm and puffed up. Serve immediately. You won't notice the bread – it will have become as one with the other ingredients.

Mushroom Brunch Soufflé

This is my version of the Sausagemeat Soufflé dish, so perfect for a brunch, for those who don't eat meat!

SERVES 6–8

6 slices of brown bread, crusts removed, and the bread cut into 1-inch/2.5-cm cubes	*2 onions, skinned and finely chopped*
3 tbsp olive oil	*A grating of nutmeg*
1½ lb/675 g mushrooms, wiped and chopped	*Salt and pepper*
	8 large eggs, beaten with 1 pt/570 ml milk
	6 oz/170 g grated cheese

Lightly oil an ovenproof dish with at least a 4-pint/2.25-litre capacity. Put the cubes of bread in the bottom. Heat the oil in a heavy-based sauté pan and cook the chopped mushrooms over a high heat till they are almost crisp – this greatly improves their flavour. Lower the heat, scoop the mushrooms out of the pan and put them in with the bread. Cook the finely chopped onions in the pan (you may need to add another spoonful of oil) till they are really soft and just beginning to turn golden at the edges. Scoop them in amongst the mushrooms. Mix the nutmeg, salt and pepper in with the eggs and milk and pour this over the bread and mushrooms. Scatter the grated cheese over the surface – it will sink in, but it doesn't matter. Cover with clingfilm and leave in the fridge overnight.

In the morning, remove the clingfilm and bake the dish in a moderate oven, 350°F/180°C/Gas Mark 4, for 45–50 minutes. It should be well puffed up and firm. Serve immediately.

Devilled Kidneys

I am quite intrigued, when I 'do' kidneys at a cooking demonstration, and ask those present who do not like kidneys to put up their hands, what a small percentage of the guests don't like them. Four out of the seven in our family absolutely love kidneys, one doesn't mind them, and two actively dislike them. Kidneys are such convenient food (like fish) because they cook so quickly. In fact, overcooked lambs' kidneys become tough and rubbery in texture, and their flavour deteriorates, too, with overcooking. Devilled kidneys are a perfect brunch dish, because they go so well with any dish containing eggs, or with bacon, sausages and black pudding.

You can core the kidneys – easiest done with a sharp pair of scissors – the night before. Kidneys bought in a butcher's shop are the best. Those prepacked in supermarkets tend to seep a lot of blood as they sit, once cored.

SERVES 6

2 oz/56 g butter and 1 tbsp sunflower oil	*2 tsp Dijon mustard*
	2 tsp medium curry powder
12 lambs' kidneys, each cut in half and the core snipped out	*1 tbsp Green Label mango chutney, trying not to include actual bits of mango*
2 tsp English mustard powder	*½ pt/285 ml double cream*
	Salt and pepper

Melt the butter and heat the oil together in a sauté pan. Over a fairly high heat cook the prepared kidneys till they just curl up, turning them over to let them cook on either side. Move them to a warm dish. Stir in the mustard powder, made-up Dijon mustard, curry powder, chutney, cream, salt and pepper. Let them all bubble briefly, then replace the kidneys in the sauce to reheat. Cook for a minute, then serve in a warm dish.

Homemade Muesli

This isn't really muesli, more a delicious crunchy cereal, good to nibble just as it is, or to eat with fresh sliced fruit at the start of a brunch.

¼ pt/140 ml sunflower oil	*6 oz/170 g bran*
½ pt/285 ml maple syrup	*4 oz/112 g sesame seeds*
1 lb/450 g porridge oats	*4 oz/112 g sunflower seeds*
(rolled oats)	*4 oz/112 g sultanas*
6 oz/170 g pinhead oatmeal	

Put the oil and maple syrup into a saucepan and heat till they are bubbling. Meanwhile, mix together the rest of the ingredients in a bowl. Mix in the bubbling oil and maple syrup, mixing very well.

Oil two baking trays, and spread out the mixture between both trays. Bake in a moderate oven, 350°F/180°C/Gas Mark 4, for 5 minutes. Stir the contents of each tray around (I find it easiest to use a fork), then cook again for 5 minutes. Stir the contents around again. Continue doing this until everything is lightly toasted – about 20–25 minutes' cooking time in total.

Take the tins out of the oven, and fork round the ingredients as they cool, otherwise they tend to stick to the trays. When they are absolutely cold, store in an airtight container.

Spicy Raisin Buns

You can cut a cross on top of these, just before baking, using a razor blade or a very sharp knife, to turn them into hot cross buns for Easter eating. They haven't got any mixed peel in them, which seems to be the part that more people dislike than like, and yet you get the citrus flavour via the grated lemon and orange rinds. As with all bread food, these freeze very well.

MAKES 12–16

1 lb/450 g wholemeal or strong plain white flour – I like to use double 0 (00 on the packet) flour from an Italian delicatessen	*1 scant tbsp dried yeast – I use Allinson's*
	½ pt/285 ml hand-hot water with 2 tsp sugar stirred in
	1 large egg, beaten
2 tsp powdered cinnamon and a good grating of nutmeg	*2 oz/56 g soft butter*
	4 oz/112 g sultanas or raisins
Black pepper, about 12 grinds of the peppermill	*Grated rinds of 1 lemon and 1 orange*

Put the flour and spices into a large mixing bowl. Stir the yeast into the sugar and water and leave in a warm place – but not on direct heat – till a head of froth forms equal in size to the liquid underneath. Mix this into the flour with the egg and soft butter and stir in the raisins and grated orange and lemon rinds. Mix well, then turn the sticky dough on to a floured surface and knead till it is not sticky. Cut the dough in half, then cut each half in half again, and continue to divide the dough like this till you have 12 or 16 bits of dough. Roll each into bun shape and put them on to a lightly oiled baking tray.

Leave in a warm place till they are twice their original size, then bake in a very hot oven, 425°F/220°C/Gas Mark 7, for 12–15 minutes – when a bun sounds hollow if tapped on the base it is cooked. Cool on a wire rack. I like them best served warm, with butter and marmalade.

Apple Spice Cake

This is baked in a 9 × 13 inch/23 × 33 cm baking tray, approximately 1½ inches/4 cm deep. The deliciously gooey cake is cut into chunky squares to serve. It can be made a couple of days before a brunch because it almost improves on keeping.

---

12 oz/340 g plain flour
2 tsp bicarbonate of soda
½ tsp salt
2 tsp cinnamon
About ½ tsp grated nutmeg
12 oz/340 g soft brown sugar
¼ pt/140 ml sunflower oil
2 large eggs, beaten
Grated rind of 1 lemon
4 oz/112 g sieved ground almonds

1 tsp vanilla essence, or several drops of extract
1½ lb/675 g good eating apples, e.g. Cox's or Granny Smith's, peeled, cored and chopped quite small
6 oz/170 g demerara sugar mixed well with 2 tsp powdered cinnamon

---

Sieve the flour, bicarbonate of soda, salt and spices into a bowl. In another bowl beat together the soft brown sugar, oil and eggs. Mix these into the sieved dry ingredients. Stir in the lemon rind, ground almonds, vanilla and apples.

Line the baking tray with baking parchment, and pour in the cake mixture. Smooth it even and bake in a moderate oven, 350°F/180°C/Gas Mark 4, for about 40–45 minutes, or till when you stick a knife in the middle it comes out only slightly sticky.

As soon as you take it out of the oven, sprinkle on the sugar and cinnamon mixture, which will stick to the hot cake surface. Cool the cake in its tin.

Iced Coffee with Cinnamon

This is a perfect brunch drink (I do hate the word beverage) for a warm summer's day. Whatever the weather, try putting half a teaspoon of powdered cinnamon into your coffee maker along with the ground coffee – cinnamon and coffee are extremely complementary flavours.

1 rounded tsp powdered cinnamon, stirred in with the amount of ground coffee that you like to make the coffee the strength you like	*continental roast beans, freshly ground, and I make it in a cafetière*
2 pts/1.1 l strong coffee – I like to make it with	*4 tsp soft brown sugar – this suits most tastes without making the iced coffee too sweet*
	1/2 pt/285 ml single cream

Stir the sugar into the hot coffee and leave to cool. When it is cold, pour it into a jug and stir in very cold single cream. If you like, add ice cubes to the jug.

Creamy Mushrooms with Croûtons

As with the Scrambled Eggs with Tomatoes and Red Peppers recipe, the croûtons in this dish are large, and could be described as fried bread. I pile the mushrooms in their nutmeg seasoned sauce in the middle of a warmed dish, with the croûtons around the edges – if you spoon the mushrooms on to the crisp croûtons and they sit for any length of time they tend to go soft. Part of the attraction of this dish is the contrast of crunchy croûtons and creamy mushroom. This is also a good dish for a brunch if you have non-meat eating guests.

SERVES 4

4 slices of thick bread, brown or white, each cut into a circle about 3 inches/8 cm in diameter	*1 1/2 lb/675 g mushrooms, wiped and stalks trimmed but not yet removed, and the mushrooms quartered (or sliced, if you prefer)*
Melted butter, to brush the bread	
2 oz/56 g butter and 1 tbsp oil	

For the sauce:
2 oz/56 g butter
2 oz/56 g flour

³/₄–1 pt/420–570 ml creamy
milk
Salt, pepper and nutmeg

Start by making the croûtons – which you can do a day in advance as they warm up very well. Cut a large circle out of each slice of bread and brush on either side with melted butter. Brush a baking tray with melted butter and bake the buttered circles of bread till they are golden brown, in a hot oven – about 5–7 minutes.

Cook the mushrooms by melting the butter and heating the oil in a heavy sauté pan and, when both are very hot, cook the quartered mushrooms till they are almost crisp – their flavour is much better if they are cooked till this point. They will absorb nearly all the butter and oil as they cook.

Make the sauce by melting the butter in a saucepan and stirring in the flour. Let this cook for a minute before stirring in the creamy milk, adding it gradually, and stirring till the sauce bubbles gently. Take the pan off the heat and season with salt, pepper and freshly grated nutmeg. Stir in the sautéed mushrooms and dish them into a warmed serving dish. Put the croûtons around the edge of the mushrooms.

Stuffed Croissants

A plate of warm stuffed croissants makes very good brunch food. You can buy such a variety of croissants these days, but the ones I like best are the Marks & Spencer's all-butter French ones. Make a filling of your choice, whether flaked smoked haddock or cod stirred into a creamy sauce, or, as in this rather richer filling, crisply cooked bacon broken into a cheese sauce.

SERVES 4

6 rashers of smoked (or unsmoked, if you prefer) bacon	*1 pt/570 ml milk*
	A pinch of salt, a grating of nutmeg, black pepper
4 croissants	*1 tsp Dijon mustard*
2 oz/56 g butter	*4 oz/112 g grated Cheddar cheese*
2 oz/56 g flour	

Grill the bacon till crisp, then chop it into small bits. Heat the croissants.

Make the sauce by melting the butter in a saucepan and stirring in the flour. Let this mixture cook for a minute before stirring in the milk, adding it gradually, and stirring continuously till the sauce bubbles gently. Take the pan off the heat, and stir in the seasonings, the mustard and the grated cheese. Stir till the cheese melts. Stir the bits of bacon into the sauce.

Split each croissant lengthwise and put them in an ovenproof dish. Spoon the filling into them – it will spill from the croissants, but it is meant to. I like to eat Grilled Tomatoes with Basil and Ginger with these bacon and cheese croissants.

Informal Lunches, Saturday Family Lunches

Lemon, Thyme and Garlic Bread

Black Olive, Sun-Dried Tomato and Garlic Bread

Cheese and Mustard Bread

Prune Bread

Sesame Toasts

Smoked Fish Florentine

Minestrone

Red Onion Soup with Balsamic Vinegar and Goats' Cheese Croûtons

Leek, Mushroom and Madeira Soup

Creamy Roast Red Pepper Soup

Tomato Tart with Cheese Pastry

Ham and Pasta Casserole

Crab Soufflé

Roast Vegetable Salad

Couscous Salad with Roast Red Onions and Peppers and Lemon and Thyme Dressing

Spinach and Mushroom Risotto

Leek and Smoked Haddock Chowder

Tomato, Goats' Cheese and Leek Tart

Ham and Bean Soup

Pheasant and Mushroom Soup

INFORMAL LUNCHES,
SATURDAY FAMILY LUNCHES

When any of our children are home for the weekend, Saturday lunch is one of my favourite times. It is the informality, and the knowledge that there is the whole of the rest of the day to enjoy, whereas Sundays can be rather a rush, what with trying to have lunch a bit earlier than we otherwise might, in order to get anyone leaving away on the road to the mainland and their various destinations south of Skye. Lunch is a meal we only ever eat with any degree of planning when there are more to the household than just me and Godfrey. Don't for a minute think that when alone either of us do without lunch! Would I? But it might just be granary toast and Marmite with grilled tomatoes, or about six days out of seven, soup, one of so very many different types.

We both love soups, and in this chapter are recipes for substantial soups which are robust, and could be described as a lunch in themselves. Soups such as the Ham and Bean one, or the Pheasant and Mushroom, or the Minestrone, or the Red Onion Soup with Balsamic Vinegar, with its Goats' Cheese Croûtons. There are recipes for breads, which when accompanying any of the soups add the final touch.

There are a couple of salad recipes, one with roast vegetables, and another based on couscous, which I love. There is a recipe for Tomato Tart with Cheese Pastry which, when accompanied by a mixed green salad, is a delicious lunch. The Crab Soufflé is a slightly more elegant lunch dish, but so convenient in that the entire thing can be made, the dish covered with clingfilm and the washing-up done, two or three hours before lunchtime, so all you need to do is to remove the clingfilm and pop the soufflé in the oven to cook. All in all, there is a great variety of ideas in this chapter for lunches for any time of the year and, hopefully, to appeal to a wide variety of tastes.

Lemon, Thyme and Garlic Bread

1 tsp sugar	*A small sprig of fresh*
2 tsp Allinson's dried yeast	*thyme, tiny leaves*
½ pt/285 ml hand-hot water	*plucked from the stalks,*
1 lb/450 g stong plain flour	*or a good pinch of dried*
½ tsp salt	*thyme*
2 cloves of garlic, peeled	*Grated rind of 1 lemon*
and chopped very finely	*2 tbsp extra virgin olive oil*

First, stir the sugar and yeast into the hand-hot water and leave in a warm place till a head of froth has formed equal in size to the liquid underneath. Then mix the yeast mixture into the sieved flour and salt along with the chopped garlic, thyme and grated lemon rind and olive oil. Mix all together well. Then tip the dough onto a floured work surface and knead till the dough is no longer sticky, but is pliant.

Lightly oil a baking tray, shape the dough into a rough sausage shape and put it on a baking tray. Leave, uncovered, till the dough has doubled in size, then bake in a very hot oven, 425°F/220°C/Gas Mark 7, for about 20 minutes. It should sound hollow when you tap its bottom.

Cool in a warm place – not in a cold place or a draught because that will cause the dough to toughen. This is very good with a variety of hot or cold soups, and with salad as an alternative to baked potatoes.

Black Olive, Sun-Dried Tomato and Garlic Bread

I realize that you can buy this type of flavoured bread in many shops, but none is as good as the bread you make yourself. It matters very much to use the best black olives – not those awful ones uniformly pitted and packed in bitter brine, but the juicy olives with their stones in, packed in herbs and a minimum of the best brine. The garlic amount may sound rather lavish, but bread seems to absorb the flavour of garlic, and I love a pronounced garlic taste. This bread is so good on its own, but it embellishes any soup, or it can be eaten with the best Brie – which is the one made by Curtis's called Bonchester Bridge – and salad, for the most perfect lunch.

MAKES 1 LARGE OR 2 SMALLER LOAVES

1 tsp sugar	*3 cloves of garlic, skinned*
2 tsp Allinson's dried yeast	*and chopped finely*
½ pt/285 ml hand-hot water	*About 6 pieces of sun-dried*
1 lb/450 g double 0 white	*tomato, chopped*
flour (00)	*About 14–18 best black*
½ tsp salt	*olives, chopped, stones*
	thrown away

Stir the sugar and yeast into the water and stand it in a warm place till a head of froth has formed the same size as the amount of liquid. Sieve the flour and salt into a bowl and stir in the garlic, chopped sun-dried tomatoes and chopped olives. Stir in the yeast liquid and mix very well.

Turn the dough on to a floured surface and knead till the dough is no longer sticky. Divide in two, if you want two smaller loaves, and knead a bit longer. Shape into oblongs and put on to a lightly oiled baking tray. Leave in a warm place till the dough has just about doubled in size, then bake in a hot oven, 425°F/220°C/Gas Mark 7, for 20 minutes – the bread should sound hollow when tapped on the base. Cool on a wire rack.

Cheese and Mustard Bread

This bread doesn't look particularly elegant, but it tastes so good. I think it is best when sliced and toasted; toasting brings out the cheese and garlic flavours – you don't notice the mustard, but its presence enhances the taste of the cheese. This is delicious when toasted and eaten (buttered) with scrambled eggs or grilled tomatoes.

MAKES 1 LARGE OR 2 SMALLER LOAVES

1 tsp sugar	*2 cloves of garlic, skinned*
2 tsp Allinson's dried yeast	*and chopped very finely*
½ pt/285 ml hand-hot water	*4 oz/112 g grated strong*
1 lb/450 g granary flour	*Cheddar cheese*
	3 tsp mustard powder
	1 tsp salt

Lightly oil a baking tray. Stir the sugar and yeast into the hand-hot water and leave in a warm place till a head of froth has formed equal to the amount of liquid. In a bowl mix together the flour, garlic, cheese, mustard and salt, and stir the frothy yeast mixture in well. Turn the dough on to a floured surface and knead well and rhythmically (this is very soothing) till the dough no longer feels sticky. At first you will wonder if the dough will incorporate the grated cheese, but it does! As you will discover. If you want two smaller loaves divide the dough in two and knead each a bit longer. Shape them into oblongs and put them on the oiled baking tray in a warm place, till more or less double the size. Then carefully put the baking tray into a hot oven, 425°F/220°C/Gas Mark 7, for 20 minutes – the bread should sound hollow when tapped on the base. Leave on a wire cooling rack.

This bread freezes as well as any other bread, which is excellently, but don't try to microwave thaw it. I think that microwave thawing renders bread dry and stale – it seems to draw out the moisture.

Prune Bread

I love this bread, especially with smoked fish dishes. Taste is a very individual thing, and I realize that this may sound odd to some of you, but do try it – leave out the walnuts, if you don't like them. Make this bread with wholemeal flour, if you prefer, but I like the double 0 white flour that I buy from Valvona & Crolla, the superb Italian delicatessen in Edinburgh. You can use strong plain white flour instead, but it's not as good as double 0.

MAKES 1 LARGER OR 2 SMALLER LOAVES

1 tsp sugar	*1 tsp salt*
2 tsp Allinson's dried yeast	*6 oz/170 g prunes (ready-*
½ pt/285 ml hand-hot water	*soaked ones), cut in bits,*
1 lb/450 g strong white flour	*stones thrown away*
– double 0 (00)	*2 oz/56 g chopped walnuts*

Lightly oil a baking tray. Stir the sugar and yeast into the water and set the bowl in a warm place till a head of froth develops equal in quantity to the liquid. Sieve the flour and salt into a bowl and add the chopped prunes – and the walnuts, if you are including them. Stir in the yeast liquid and mix well. Turn the dough on to a floured surface and knead until the dough is no longer sticky – about 5 minutes. Either divide into two pieces, knead each a bit longer, then form each into oblongs and put them on the oiled baking tray in a warm place till they have just about doubled in size; or form one large oblong, and put that on the baking tray. Bake in a hot oven, 425°F/220°C/Gas Mark 7, for about 20 minutes. The bread is cooked when it sounds hollow when you tap it on the base. Cool it on a wire rack, but not in a draught – that toughens the bread, tempting though it sometimes is to try to fast-cool it. This freezes as well as any other bread – extremely well.

Sesame Toasts

These are extremely useful. They can either be cut in strips, as in the recipe, or they can be cut in rounds, big or small, using scone cutters. In rounds, they can be used as the base for a wide variety of toppings, either, in the larger size, as a simple main course to be eaten in fingers, or, in the smaller versions, to accompany soups. Some of the sesame seeds will fall off as they bake, but most will stay on the toasts provided that you melt the butter and brush the bread with that, rather than trying to take a short cut and spread with soft butter, which – I don't understand why – seems to make the sesame seeds fall off to a much greater extent.

---

6 slices of thick-cut day-old
bread, crusts cut off
2 oz/56 g butter, melted

5–6 oz/140 g sesame seeds,
mixed well with 1 tsp salt

Brush a baking tray with melted butter. Cut the crustless bread into strips, each about 1 inch/2.5 cm wide. Brush each on either side with melted butter. Press the butter-brushed bread on either side in the sesame and salt. Bake in a hot oven till they are golden brown – about 8–10 minutes. You may need to turn the baking tray around as they cook – most ovens cook unevenly. Bake at oven temperature 425°F/220°C/Gas Mark 7. You can freeze them, but warm them up before serving them. They really are nicest made and eaten on the same day.

Smoked Fish Florentine

Eggs Florentine is a classic dish of puréed spinach with poached eggs and the whole covered with a good cheesy béchamel sauce. But fish Florentine is more delicious by far – I must admit that I have never been fond of eggs which aren't hardboiled, so that is why I tend to make fishy Florentines. I prefer to use smoked fish, and to microwave the baby leaf spinach I find in Marks & Spencer so conveniently – unless I am in Perth, where I was told that baby spinach isn't ever sold! I was told this by a member of staff in dear old Marks & Spencer and I can only suppose that Perthshire residents get their iron from other sources – or they travel to Edinburgh for their baby spinach.

SERVES 6

2 lb/900 g smoked haddock	*4 oz/112 g butter*
2 pt/1.1 l milk	*Salt, pepper and nutmeg*
3 bags of baby spinach, each	*2 oz/56 g flour*
microwaved according to	*1 pt/570 ml of the fish milk*
the instructions on the	*Pepper and nutmeg*
packet; or, if you haven't	*4 oz/112 g grated Cheddar*
– yet! – got a microwave	*cheese – keep about 1 oz/*
oven, steam the spinach	*28 g of this aside*
just till it wilts	

Start by preparing and cooking the fish. Feel the raw fish on a board, removing all bones. This is so much easier to do when the fish is raw, rather than later when it is cooked. Put it into a saucepan with the milk and, over moderate heat, bring the milk to just simmering point. Cool the fish in the milk. Then strain off 1 pint/570 ml for making into the cheese sauce – keep the rest of the milk for making into soup at a later date.

With a sharp knife chop the cooked spinach, by whichever means, and cut in 2 oz/56 g of the butter. I prefer chopped spinach rather than puréed. Chop in the salt, pepper and nutmeg. Butter an ovenproof dish with a 3–4 pint/1.7–2.3 litre capacity. Put the chopped seasoned spinach into this and spread it evenly over the base of the dish.

Flake the cooked fish and put it on top of the spinach. Make the sauce by melting the remaining butter in a saucepan and stirring in the flour. Let this cook for a minute before stirring in the reserved fish milk – I use a wire whisk for a really smooth sauce – stirring till the sauce simmers. Draw the pan off the heat and season the sauce with pepper and a grating of nutmeg – no more salt will be needed, as the smoked fish will add enough saltiness for most palates. Stir in three-quarters of the grated cheese. Pour this over the fish and spinach, and sprinkle the rest of the grated cheese over the surface. Reheat under a hot grill, till the grated cheese melts.

If you prepare the Florentine ahead, reheat in a moderate oven till the cheese on top melts – about 20–25 minutes at 350°F/180°C/ Gas Mark 4.

Minestrone

I make no apology for including this recipe in this book. It is in my first book, *Seasonal Cooking*, which was published thirteen years ago, and more recently in *Suppers*, but it is such an everlasting favourite, and if I had to choose a lunch-time main course above all others for an informal lunch it would be Minestrone. It has so much going for it – it tastes so good above all else, it is very good for us in that it contains nothing rich at all – if you forget about the freshly grated Parmesan cheese which is such a necessary accompaniment! – and it's packed full of vegetables which some children wouldn't eat if served individually, but all children I've ever come across seem to love Minestrone and all therein contained. And it freezes beautifully, too. It is very filling and sustaining – it's just perfect. If you don't eat meat, just leave out the smoked bacon and use vegetable stock instead of chicken stock.

SERVES ABOUT 8, DEPENDING ON APPETITES

4 tbsp olive oil

2 onions, skinned and chopped quite finely

6 rashers of smoked bacon (or unsmoked, if you prefer), most of the fat removed and the bacon neatly chopped

2 cloves of garlic, skinned

and chopped

2 carrots, peeled and diced

3 potatoes, peeled and diced

3 sticks of celery, washed, trimmed and sliced thinly

About 1 lb/450 g white cabbage, or Brussels sprouts, trimmed and sliced thinly

¼ pt/140 ml red wine

2 pt/1.1 l chicken stock

2 cans (14 oz/400 g) chopped
tomatoes

Salt and freshly ground
black pepper

A couple of pinches of sugar

2 tsp pesto

1 can (15 oz/420 g) baked
beans, preferably Heinz

In a large, heavy-based saucepan, heat the oil and add the chopped onions and the bacon. Cook, stirring occasionally, for about 5 minutes – till the onion is soft and just beginning to turn golden at the edges. Then stir in the chopped garlic, diced carrots and potatoes, sliced celery and sliced cabbage or Brussels sprouts. Cook for a further few minutes, then pour in the red wine, stock and tomatoes. Season with salt, pepper, sugar and pesto, and bring the soup slowly to simmering point. Cover with a lid and simmer very gently for about 1 hour. Stir in the contents of the can of baked beans, and serve.

Alternatively, you can cool completely, then add the baked beans and reheat to serve. It keeps perfectly well, covered, in the fridge for two days. Or freeze it. Allow 24–36 hours to thaw.

Red Onion Soup with Balsamic Vinegar and Goats' Cheese Croûtons

I ate this soup – or one similar – in the Malmaison Hotel in Leith, at an excellent bar lunch. I thought it would be fun and good to experiment with the theme, which is a variation on the Onion Soup with Toasted Cheese in *Seasonal Cooking*. I do love the mild flavour of red onions, and their caramelizing as they sauté is complemented by the balsamic vinegar (but you do have to beware not to use too much). I love balsamic vinegar, used sparingly, and I tend to include a teaspoonful or two in most casseroles of meat or game.

The goats' cheese is far better than Cheddar cheese would be with these flavours.

SERVES 6

---

1 oz/28 g butter	*canned consommé – or*
2 tbs oil	*good vegetable stock*
6 fairly large red-skinned	*2 tsp balsamic vinegar*
onions, each skinned and	*12 slices from a stick of*
sliced as finely as you can	*French bread*
1–2 cloves of garlic, skinned	*8 oz/225 g soft goats' cheese*
and finely chopped	*Black pepper*
1½–2 pt/850–1100 ml beef	*Salt*
stock – you can use	*A grating of nutmeg*

Heat the butter and oil together in a large saucepan, and stir in the red onions. It will look a lot, but as they cook they reduce right down in quantity. Cook them over a moderate heat, stirring from time to time, for 12–15 minutes. Stir in the garlic and cook for a further 2–3 minutes, then stir in the stock and balsamic vinegar. Simmer all together, with the pan half covered with its lid, for about 30 minutes.

While the soup cooks, prepare the croûtons by spreading goats' cheese on each slice of bread, grinding black pepper on top, then grilling for 45–60 seconds – just till the surface begins to speckle brown. Keep the croûtons warm in a low oven.

Before serving, season the soup with salt, pepper and a grating of nutmeg. Ladle it into bowls or soup plates, and put two goats' cheese croûtons on each serving.

Leek, Mushroom and Madeira Soup

These flavours go together extremely well. This soup has the added bonus of being very low in calories, yet it is satisfying to eat. As with all soups, the stock is all-important. I prefer to use chicken stock, but a good vegetable stock is a close second.

SERVES 6–8

3 tbsp olive or sunflower oil	*2 pts/1.1 l good stock,*
+ 1 oz/28 g butter	*chicken or vegetable*
1 lb/450 g mushrooms, each	*3 oz/84 g long grain white*
wiped and chopped quite	*rice, e.g. Basmati*
small	*Salt and pepper*
6 leeks, each washed well,	*A grating of nutmeg*
trimmed and sliced thinly	*¼ pt/140 ml Madeira*

Heat the oil and melt the butter together in a saucepan and cook the mushrooms till they almost squeak – this improves their taste no end. Scoop them out of the pan and add the leeks to the pan. You may need to add another tablespoon of oil, the mushrooms do rather tend to absorb it. Cook the leeks for a couple of minutes, then replace the mushrooms and stir in the stock, rice, salt, pepper and a grating of nutmeg.

Simmer the soup very gently for about 15–20 minutes. Just before ladling it into the bowls, stir in the Madeira.

Creamy Roast Red Pepper Soup

This soup is delicious served hot or chilled. It isn't a very thick soup – I loathe using flour to thicken a soup – but it is intense in its flavour. Roasting vegetables gives such a depth of taste, and how I love it! The colour of this soup is particularly attractive. The Black Olive, Sun-Dried Tomato and Garlic Bread is ideal as an accompaniment for this soup.

SERVES 6

3 tbsp olive oil	1¹/₂–2 pts/850–110 ml good
2 onions, skinned and	chicken or vegetable stock
chopped	Salt and pepper
6 red peppers	A squeeze of lemon juice
2 cloves of garlic, skinned	A swirl of crème fraîche for
and chopped	the garnish for each
2 tbsp olive oil – for roast-	serving
ing the peppers and garlic	

Heat the oil in a saucepan and cook the chopped onions for 5–7 minutes, stirring from time to time, till they are beginning to turn golden at the edges. Meanwhile, heat a grill to red-hot and put the peppers under it, turning them, till they char with great black blisters. Put them into a polythene bag for 10 minutes. Their skins will then slip off. Cut each in half and remove their stalks and seeds. Chop the flesh roughly.

Put the chopped peppers and garlic together on a roasting tray, and mix well with 2 tablespoons of olive oil. Roast in a hot oven, 425°F/220°C/Gas Mark 7 for 10 minutes. Take out of the oven, and stir into the onions in the saucepan. Stir in the stock, and season with salt, pepper and a squeeze of lemon juice. Simmer all the ingredients together, very gently, for 10 minutes. Cool, and liquidize the soup to a velvety smooth texture.

Either chill in a bowl in the fridge, or reheat gently, to serve. Whether you serve the soup hot or cold, put a teaspoonful of crème fraîche in each serving.

Tomato Tart with Cheese Pastry

This is best made in the summer when tomatoes taste their best. The cheese pastry has its flavour accentuated by the mustard powder – but you don't actually taste the mustard. It's a slightly rich but utterly delicious savoury tart, only needing a green salad to go with it.

SERVES 6

For the pastry:

4 oz/112 g butter hard from the fridge, cut into bits

3 oz/84 g grated Cheddar cheese

6 oz/170 g plain flour

Salt and pepper

2 tsp mustard powder

For the filling:

6 tomatoes, skinned, halved

and the seeds removed, and the flesh roughly chopped

1–2 cloves of garlic, skinned and finely chopped (optional)

2 large eggs + 2 large egg yolks

1/2 pt/285 ml single cream

Salt and pepper

Basil leaves, torn up

Put all the ingredients for the pastry into a food processor and whiz till fine. Pat this firmly around the sides and base of the 9-inch/23-cm flan dish and put the dish into the fridge for at least an hour. Then bake in a moderate oven, 350°F/180°C/Gas Mark 4, till the pastry is pale golden. If you notice the pastry slipping down the sides of the dish as it cooks, press it back up the sides with the back of a metal spoon and continue to cook for a few more minutes. The cooking will take about 20–25 minutes.

Put the chopped tomatoes on the cooked pastry base, and scatter on the garlic if used. Beat together the eggs and yolks, gradually mixing in the cream. Season with salt and pepper and pour this over the tomatoes. Scatter the basil leaves over everything.

Bake in a moderate oven till the filling is just firm, about 20 minutes. Serve warm.

Ham and Pasta Casserole

Pasta is such a favourite in our family that we seem to eat it in one form or another several times a week. This is a variation on the old macaroni cheese. The better the ham you use the better will be the end result – this is a useful dish to use up left-over ham from a roast ham. I prefer to use a short type of pasta, like bows or shells, for this dish.

SERVES 6–8

1 lb/450 g pasta bows
2 tbsp olive oil
2 oz/56 g butter and 1 tbsp olive oil
2 medium onions, skinned and finely chopped
1 clove of garlic, skinned and finely chopped
2 fairly level tbsp flour

1 pt/570 ml milk
Salt and freshly ground black pepper
A grating of nutmeg
4 oz/112 g grated Cheddar or Lancashire cheese
6–8 oz/170–225 g ham, cut in strips, any fat or gristle removed

Boil the pasta in plenty of salted water till you can stick your thumbnail through a bit – drain, and toss in 2 tablespoons of olive oil to prevent it sticking together.

Meanwhile, make the sauce by melting the butter and heating the olive oil together in a saucepan. Add the chopped onions and cook over a moderate heat till the onions are really soft and just turning golden brown at the edges. Add the chopped garlic, and stir in the flour. Cook for a minute, then gradually add the milk, stirring all the time till the sauce simmers. Draw the pan off the heat and stir in the seasonings, and half the grated cheese. Stir in the cooked pasta and the ham.

Pour into an ovenproof dish, sprinkle the remaining cheese over the surface, and pop under a hot grill till the cheese melts and turns golden. Serve with a salad.

Crab Soufflé

This is for a rather more grown-up and slightly more sophisticated lunch, but the reason this dish is in this chapter is that it is so straight-forward and simple to make. Crab is really very filling, and if the amount of crab in the recipe seems a bit mean to you, it is because a little goes a long way.

SERVES 6

Butter for greasing	*A pinch of salt and plenty of*
Parmesan cheese	*freshly ground black*
2 oz/56 g butter	*pepper*
2 level tbsp flour	*A grating of nutmeg*
1 tsp mustard powder	*A dash of Tabasco sauce*
¾ pt/430 ml full fat milk	*5 large eggs, separated*
(much nicer than	*1 lb/450 g crabmeat, and I*
skimmed for this dish)	*prefer half white and half*
2 tbsp dry sherry	*brown*

Butter a large soufflé dish, or any ovenproof dish (such as Pyrex), and dust out the dish with freshly grated Parmesan cheese.

Melt the butter in a large saucepan and stir in the flour and mustard. Let this cook for a minute before stirring in the milk, adding it gradually and stirring all the time till the sauce simmers. Draw the pan off the heat and stir in the sherry, salt, pepper, nutmeg and Tabasco. Beat in the yolks, one by one. Cover the surface of the sauce with damp greaseproof paper and leave to cool – the paper will prevent a skin forming; if you prefer you can use clingfilm instead of the greaseproof. When it is cold, beat in the crabmeat – you can do all this the previous day if it is more convenient for you.

In a clean bowl whisk the whites till they are very stiff and, with a large metal spoon, fold them quickly and thoroughly through the crab mixture. Pour and scrape this into the prepared soufflé dish and bake in a hot oven, 425°F/220°C/Gas Mark 7, for 30–35 minutes, then serve immediately, with a green salad.

Roast Vegetable Salad

This is a warm salad and is very good with either the Black Olive, Sun-Dried Tomato and Garlic Bread or the Lemon, Thyme and Garlic Bread as accompaniment. Roasting vegetables need careful watching as they roast – there is a fine line between roasting and burning. A touch of charring here and there is perfectly acceptable, but any overall surface blackening doesn't make for good eating! Don't be fooled by recipes which tell you to wrap vegetables for 'roasting' in foil – roasting means that the heat should be direct. When the vegetables are foil-wrapped they steam within their parcel. This is simple, but delicious.

SERVES 6

6 small red-skinned onions,	*3 aubergines*
or 3 larger ones	*6 cloves of garlic, skinned*
6 courgettes, as similar in	*8 tbsp very good olive oil*
size as possible	*3 tsp balsamic vinegar*
6 red peppers	*Salt and pepper*
3 yellow peppers	*Assorted salad leaves*

Line a roasting tin with foil – try not to mass the vegetables in the roasting tin, they need space for their roasting. Skin the onions and if using the large ones, quarter them. Cut the ends off the courgettes and slice each in quarters lengthways. Cut each pepper in half and put under a red-hot grill till the skins char in black blisters, then put the pepper halves into a large polythene bag for 10 minutes; their skins should then peel off easily. Slice each pepper in half in fat strips. Cut both ends off the aubergines, and cut each in half lengthways. Cut each half in four strips. Chop the skinned garlic roughly.

Mix all the vegetables with olive oil, so each is coated with oil. Put them on the foil in a hot oven, 425°F/220°C/Gas Mark 7, for 10 minutes. Turn them over and carefully baste with olive oil and replace them in the oven for a further 10 minutes. Stick a fork in a piece of aubergine and test for tenderness – it should feel soft. If it is, take the roasting tin out of the oven, if it isn't, give the vegetables a further 5 minutes' cooking time.

When you take the vegetables out of the oven, carefully stir in amongst them the balsamic vinegar, salt and pepper. Distribute the roast vegetables on to six large warmed plates, on which you have arranged a bed of assorted lettuce leaves, and spoon over each plateful any olive oil and vegetable juices from the foil.

Couscous Salad with Roast Red Onions and Peppers and Lemon and Thyme Dressing

This is a most delicious salad whether you eat meat or not – I find that we, along with very many other families in Britain today, eat far less meat than we used to. When cooking couscous I prefer not to buy the quick-cook stuff. As with rice, I find the flavour of the couscous which needs longer cooking so much better. I like to surround this salad with barely steamed sugarsnap peas and thin beans – it looks pretty and tastes good all together.

SERVES 6

4 tbsp olive oil – I use extra virgin olive oil

3 red-skinned onions, skinned and chopped quite small and neatly

12 oz/340 g couscous

2 cloves of garlic, skinned and finely chopped (optional)

3 red peppers, skinned as described on the previous recipe and chopped quite neatly

For the dressing:

Finely grated rind of 1 lemon (well washed and dried before grating)

A sprig of thyme, its tiny leaves stripped off the stalks

A pinch of salt and a good grinding of black pepper

Juice of half a lemon

6 tbsp best extra virgin olive oil

Heat the olive oil in a wide heavy-based sauté pan and add the chopped onions. Cook for about 4–5 minutes, stirring from time to time, then stir in the couscous and garlic. Cook, again stirring occasionally, for a further 5 minutes, then pour in 2 pints/1.1 litres of water. Stir as the couscous cooks over a moderate heat. The water will be absorbed. When the couscous is quite firm – as opposed to sloppy – stir in the chopped skinned red peppers and the ingredients of the dressing.

Let the couscous cool, forking the mixture through from time to time. It will absorb the flavours of the dressing as it cools. To serve, heap up the couscous on a large serving plate and surround it with barely steamed sugarsnap peas, or with assorted lettuce leaves if you prefer.

Spinach and Mushroom Risotto

Risotto is one of the most popular of all our family dishes. As with many dishes in this chapter and in other chapters, this risotto is eminently suitable for those who don't eat meat or fish, providing that a good vegetarian stock is substituted for the chicken stock of my choice. Any homemade stock is preferable to stock cubes and water, but if you do have to resort to cubes, those with no additives such as Kallo or Friggs are far superior to those which are heavily laced with monosodium glutamate, which gives a syrupy sameness to all the various flavoured cubes.

SERVES 6–8

4–5 tbsp good olive oil (I use extra virgin, usually Berio, for cooking)

2 onions, skinned and neatly chopped

1–2 cloves of garlic, skinned and finely chopped (optional)

1 lb/450 g mushrooms, each wiped and chopped (you can use wild mushrooms, I use our chanterelles and horns of plenty when they are in season)

1 lb/450 g Arborio rice (or similar risotto rice)

¼ pt/140 ml dry white wine

2½–3 pt/1.4–1.7 l chicken or
  vegetable stock

A couple of pinches of
  saffron (optional, but
  delicious)

Salt and pepper

3 oz/84 g baby spinach
  leaves, torn into bits

Freshly grated Parmesan
  cheese for handing round
  to sprinkle on the risotto

Heat the oil in a wide-based and fairly deep sauté pan and cook the chopped onions for several minutes, till they are transparent. Stir in the chopped garlic and the mushrooms and the rice, all together, and mix well, so that pretty well each grain of rice has a coating of olive oil. This will take several minutes' stirring around. Then stir in the dry white wine, and after that, in stages, a small amount at a time, the stock, stirring from time to time as the risotto cooks very gently. The risotto rice has the ability to absorb quantities of liquid and yet retain the individual grain shape. When you first add the stock, add the saffron, too, if you are using it. Season with salt and pepper, and lastly stir in the torn up spinach which will wilt in the heat of the risotto.

In this country risotto tends to be too stiff; it is so much nicer slightly on the sloppy side, so watch out for this. Taste, and season with salt and pepper as you like it. Serve with the freshly grated Parmesan cheese handed round separately.

Leek and Smoked Haddock Chowder

I have only fairly recently realized just how good are leeks with any smoked fish. This soup is a meal in itself. I like to liquidize half the potato and leeks in their fishy milk and water, and then leave the rest of the soup in chunks of potato and sliced leeks, with the cooked fish flaked through. This gives a fairly thick base to the soup, yet provides a contrasting texture with the bits of fish, potato and leek at the same time. The chopped parsley must be added at the last moment, to preserve its colour and flavour.

SERVES 6-8

*1¹/₂ lb/675 g smoked
   haddock (or smoked cod)*
*3 pt/1.7 l milk and water
   mixed – I leave the ratio
   up to you*
*3 tbsp sunflower oil + 1 oz/
   28 g butter*
*1 onion, skinned and neatly
   chopped*

*3 good sized leeks, each
   washed well and
   trimmed, and sliced
   about 1 inch/2.5 cm thick*
*5–6 potatoes, peeled and
   chopped neatly*
Plenty of black pepper
A grating of nutmeg
*2 tbsp finely chopped
   parsley*

Feel the fish on a board, and remove all bones – it is much easier to do this before the fish is cooked, I have discovered. With a very sharp knife, remove the skin from the fish. Put the fish in a saucepan with the milk and water, and over a moderate heat let the liquid come to the simmering point. Take the pan off the heat and let the fish cool in the liquid.

Meanwhile, heat the oil and melt the butter together in a large saucepan. Cook the chopped onion for a couple of minutes, then stir in the sliced leeks and chopped potatoes. Cook for about 10 minutes – you will need to stir fairly frequently to prevent it all from sticking. Season with pepper and nutmeg, and pour in the strained fish liquid. Cook this gently, with the liquid barely simmering, till the pieces of potato are soft when you squish them against the side of the saucepan with the back of your wooden spoon.

Cool the soup a bit, then liquidize half the contents of the saucepan and return the smooth soup to the pan. Flake the cooked fish and stir that, too, into the soup. Taste, add more pepper if you think it is needed, and reheat gently before serving. Just before you ladle the soup into the bowls or soup plates, stir the chopped parsley through the soup.

Tomato, Goats' Cheese and Leek Tart

The flavours of the tomatoes, goats' cheese and leeks go together so very well that this tart is a great favourite of mine. I use creamy goats' cheese, crumbled. I never used to like goats' cheese until I ate it hot for the first time, and now it is one of my most sought-after food items – but I still prefer it hot to cold.

SERVES 6–8

For the pastry:

4 oz/112 g butter, hard from the fridge, cut into bits

6 oz/170 g plain flour

1 tsp icing sugar

½ tsp salt and a good grinding of pepper

For the filling:

2 tbsp olive oil

4 leeks, washed, trimmed and sliced thinly

4 oz/112 g soft goats' cheese, crumbled

2 large eggs + 2 large egg yolks

½ pt/285 ml single cream

A pinch of salt (the cheese will be quite salty) and plenty of pepper

5 tomatoes, skinned, each cut in half, de-seeded and sliced into thin strips

Put all the ingredients for the pastry into a food processor and whiz till the mixture resembles fine crumbs. Pat this firmly around the sides and base of a 9-inch/23-cm flan dish. Put the dish into the fridge for at least an hour, then bake in a moderate oven, 350°F/180°C/Gas Mark 4, for 20–25 minutes. If the pastry looks at though it is slipping down the sides as it cooks, press it back up using the back of a metal spoon.

Heat the oil in a sauté or frying pan and cook the leeks over a moderate heat till they are soft. This will only take about 5 minutes at the most – leeks cook more quickly than onions. Scoop them into the cooked pastry base. Distribute the crumbled goats' cheese over the leeks. Beat together the eggs, yolks and cream and season with the pinch of salt and pepper. Pour this in amongst the leeks and goats' cheese. Arrange the strips of tomato on the runny top.

Carefully put the flan dish into a moderate oven (as for the pastry) and cook till the custard filling is just set when you gently shake the dish, about 20 minutes. Serve warm or cold – I think it is nicer warm.

Ham and Bean Soup

This is a sustaining meal in a soup. It needs long, slow cooking and is therefore very convenient in that it has to be made in advance. I prefer to use a smoked ham hock, but it can be very salty so I soak it overnight and throw away the water before simmering it with the other ingredients of the soup.

Serves 6–8

1 ham hock, smoked or unsmoked, whichever you prefer

1 lb/450 g haricot beans, soaked overnight

2 onions, skinned and neatly chopped

2 cloves of garlic, skinned and chopped finely

3 leeks, washed, trimmed and thinly sliced

2 sticks of celery, washed, trimmed and thinly sliced

4 pt/2.3 l water

4 medium to large potatoes, peeled and diced

Pepper to season

Salt, if needed

Put the soaked ham hock and the beans into a large saucepan with the onions, garlic, leeks and celery. Add the water and simmer very gently, with the pan uncovered, for 2 hours. Then let the soup cool. Skim off any fat from the surface. Cut the meat off the ham hock and throw away the bone and fat. Add the potatoes to the soup and simmer for a further hour. Put the cut-up ham meat into the soup 10 minutes before serving, and at the same time check the seasoning – add pepper, and salt only if you think it is needed.

Pheasant and Mushroom Soup

In the autumn and winter, when pheasants are plentiful and can be bought so easily these days by those who don't live in the country and have access to a supply of pheasants anyway, it is good to make the most of these birds. Pheasants are only mildly gamey in their taste, and their flavour combines very well with mushrooms. This soup has a small amount of Madeira which further enhances the taste of the pheasant and mushroom combination. The rice adds substance and makes this a meal type of soup.

SERVES 6–8

1 pheasant, as much fat cut off as possible	*2 onions, skinned and chopped neatly*
2 onions, cut in half (skin on)	*4 oz/112 g long grain rice, such as Basmati*
2 carrots	
2 sticks of celery	*1½ lb/675 g mushrooms, wiped and chopped quite small*
4–6 cloves	
1 tsp rock salt and several black peppercorns	*2 pt/1.1 l pheasant stock*
	¼ pt/140 ml Madeira
2 tbsp olive oil	*Salt and pepper to taste*

Wash the pheasant and put it into a large saucepan with the onions, carrots, celery, cloves, salt and peppercorns. Cover with 3 pints/1.7 litres of cold water and bring slowly to simmering point. Cover the pan with a lid and simmer all together very gently for 2 hours. If you have an Aga or a Rayburn you can do this inside, rather than on top of the cooker. Let it all cool, then take the pheasant out of the stock and cut off the meat, into small pieces. Strain the stock.

Make the soup by heating the oil and adding the chopped onions. Cook over a moderate heat for several minutes, then add the rice. Cook for a further couple of minutes, stirring, then add the chopped mushrooms and the stock. Simmer gently for 45 minutes, stirring occasionally. Add the cut-up pheasant meat and the Madeira ten minutes before serving, and at the same time check the taste and season accordingly.

Sunday Lunches

Game Pudding with Lemon Suet Crust

Steak, Kidney and Mushroom Pie

Roast Pork Loin with Tomato and Vermouth Gravy and Apple and Thyme Sauce

Roast Lamb with (a) Rosemary and Apple Jelly, (b) Mint Jelly

Roast Beef with (a) Horseradish Cream, (b) Pink Peppercorn Sauce

Roast Chicken with Creamy Saffron and Lemon Sauce

Roast Venison with Port and Redcurrant Jelly Gravy

Roast Rack of Lamb with a Herb Crust

Roast Duck with Apple and Cream Gravy

Steamed Leeks in White Sauce

Sautéed Onions in White Sauce

Braised Cabbage with Nutmeg

Braised Celery

Purée of Garden Peas with Applemint

Vegetable Pie with Lemon Grass and a Crisp Crust

SUNDAY LUNCHES

I was dismayed, not to say incredulous, to read an article in one of the Sunday broadsheets a couple of years ago stating that the traditional Sunday lunch was a thing of the past. The writer then gave the cost of rib of beef which, even allowing for the indisputable fact that such a cut is an expensive purchase, was at least double what I have ever paid for a joint. I felt that the writer was, in fact, out to damn the future of the Sunday lunch as it has been known, traditionally, in Great Britain, for very many years, and which, if I have anything to do with it, will be a part of our lives for very many years to come!

Sunday lunch is still a feature of a great many households, thank goodness. It is a time when most families reverse their usual eating trend and eat their main meal in the middle of the day. It is a time when, not withstanding the alteration in the Sunday trading laws, many families take an opportunity to gather together, using the occasion as a chance to communicate and catch up on events in one another's lives. It is an invaluable time. Sunday lunch is also an excellent time to entertain. An invitation to lunch on a Sunday is especially good for the elderly, who prefer not to go out at night and tend to eat rather more in the middle of the day than at night anyway, and for those who may have to travel some distance – such travel is much easier in the day than at night. Sunday lunch is also an opportunity for those who live alone, or who number two or three in their household, to get together with others and enjoy a roast joint of meat, an item of food which would otherwise be impractical.

One or two things have to be taken into consideration when planning what to eat for lunch on a Sunday. The most important is for churchgoers. The time of the service does determine the choice of main course. If you are in church when the joint should be going into the oven, there is no point in planning a roast meat for a main course. The alternatives are delicious and involve less last-minute cooking. A Steak and Kidney Pie, for example, whose flavour is enhanced by adding mushrooms. Or a Game Pudding, with a suet crust, which can be safely left to steam either in the oven (turned low) in a foil-enclosed baking tin with water, or in a covered saucepan on top of the cooker, on a gentle heat, provided that you top up the pan with water just before you leave for church.

There are suggestions for suitable sauces and jellies to accompany the various roast meats in this chapter, and there are also suggestions for vegetables which I think are particularly good with roast meats and pies.

Game Pudding with Lemon Suet Crust

SERVES 6

For the suet crust:
12 oz/340 g self-raising flour
6 oz/170 g shredded suet
Grated rind of 1 well
    washed and dried lemon
Salt and pepper
For the filling:
1½ lb/675 g game meat –
    hare, old grouse, venison,
    or a mixture, cut off the
carcase and cut into neat
pieces as nearly equal in
size as possible
2 tbsp flour
Salt and pepper
1 onion, skinned and
    chopped finely and neatly
1 pt/570 ml water and red
    wine or port – I leave the
    ratio up to you
1 tbsp redcurrant jelly

Mix together the pastry ingredients and stir in enough cold water to mix to a dough – about ¼ pint/140 ml. Roll out two-thirds of the dough and line a large pudding bowl with it – a boilable plastic bowl with a snap on lid is the ideal – capacity 3 pints/1.7 litres. The pastry won't fill it.

Mix together well the pieces of game, flour, seasoning and chopped onion. Pack this into the pastry-lined bowl. Measure half the water and wine (or port) into a small saucepan and stir in the redcurrant jelly. Heat till the jelly dissolves, then mix it with the rest of the liquid and pour this into the game mixture.

Roll out the remaining pastry into a circle to fit on top of the game. Cut a circle of baking parchment to fit on top, making a small pleat in the middle of its diameter. Snap on the lid and put the bowl in a large pan with water coming halfway up the sides of the bowl. Cover the pan with a lid, and bring the water in the pan to a gently simmering point. Cook like this, with the water barely simmering, for 3½–4 hours. Check the level of the water from time to time.

To reheat, steam for a further 2 hours. If you intend to serve the pudding after one steaming, steam for 5 hours.

Have a jug of hot water or stock to hand – game consommé is the best for this – to top up the liquid level inside the pudding as you spoon out its content.

Steak, Kidney and Mushroom Pie

Steak and kidney is a combination made in heaven, but it is enhanced by the flavour of the mushrooms. It might be worth mentioning for any first-time steak and kidney cooks that you can only use ox kidney in the long and slow cooking that is needed by a pie or pudding. It is perfectly safe to use ox kidney providing you ask your butcher as to its origins. Faith in your butcher is vital! If you use lambs' kidneys the flavour is bordering on the revolting once they have cooked for the length of time necessary.

SERVES 6

---

2 lb/900 g beef steak – stewing or rump

1 lb/450 g ox kidney

2 rounded tbsp flour

Salt and plenty of freshly ground black pepper

3 tbsp sunflower oil, use more if necessary – it depends what you brown

the meat in, non-stick or otherwise

1 onion, skinned and very finely chopped

1 lb/450 g mushrooms, wiped and cut in quarters, stalks trimmed but not removed

1 can lager + 1 pt/570 ml   *Milk, to brush the pastry*
stock, vegetable or beef   *with, or 1 beaten egg*
1 lb/450 g puff pastry

Trim the steak and kidney of fat or gristle and cut the meat into
1-inch/2.5-cm bits. You will have to cut the kidney as you can, but
try to make the bits as uniform in size as possible. Toss the cut-up
meat and kidney in the flour, salt and pepper.

Heat the oil and brown the meat and kidney in small amounts,
making sure that each is well browned before removing it to a warm
plate and browning the rest. Next, cook the chopped onion, till it is
transparent. Then scoop it into the browned meat. You may need
to add more oil, but turn up the heat and brown the mushrooms
very well – the more they cook, till they are almost crisp, the better
will be their flavour. Then return the browned meat, kidney and
onion to the saucepan or casserole and stir in the lager and stock,
stirring till the sauce around the meat comes to boiling point. Cover
the pan or casserole with a lid, and cook in a moderate oven, 350°F/
180°C/Gas Mark 4, for 45 minutes.

Take it out of the oven and pour the meat into a pie dish. Leave
to cool before rolling out the pastry and covering the pie as neatly as
you can. Decorate the pastry with roses or how you like, and press a
fork around the edges of the pie. Brush with either milk or beaten
egg. Slash the top of the pastry in several places – this is important,
to let any steam accumulating as the pastry cooks escape. Bake in a
hot oven, 425°F/220°C/Gas Mark 7, for 15 minutes, then reduce
the heat to moderate and cook for a further 20–25 minutes, till the
pastry is well puffed up and golden brown. Cook the pie, not
straight from the fridge, but from having been in room temperature
for an hour. You can cover it and prepare it for cooking several
hours in advance, but you will need to give it longer cooking time if
you cook it straight from the fridge.

Roast Pork Loin with Tomato and Vermouth Gravy and Apple and Thyme Sauce

The difference between mass-produced pork and free or freer range pork – where the pigs have been able to wander about in fields and are fed in a less growth-intensive way – is vast. The taste is better, but so is the texture of the meat. The best way I can describe it is being less close-grained in texture, far, far better to eat in every way. We buy loins of pork with the crackling on. I find the world is divided into people who love crackling (I'm one) and those who really dislike it. They just don't need to have any! It is many years ago now since a Canadian friend taught me how very good pork gravy is flavoured with tomato purée and vermouth, and I personally love apple sauce with pork, but only made with sautéed and very finely chopped onion, and well seasoned with thyme.

SERVES 6–8

A piece of loin weighing about 6 lb/2.7kg – I love having leftover pork to have with salad and baked potatoes or new potatoes, depending on the time of year, the following day.

I dislike any meat cooked rare with the exception of beef. I roast pork in a hot oven, 425°F/220°C/Gas Mark 7, for 40 minutes then turn the heat down to 400°F/200°C/Gas Mark 6 for the remainder of the cooking time. I give the pork 20 minutes per pound weight with about 15 minutes over. As with any roast meats, the pork is best left to stand in a very low temperature oven once cooked, for 10–15 minutes. This lets the juice settle, and makes carving easier.

Tomato and Vermouth Gravy

Either make this in the roasting tin, or pour and scrape the pork juices into a saucepan.

---

1 rounded tbsp flour
1¹/₄–1¹/₂ pt/700–840 ml
  vegetable stock
3 tsp tomato purée

¹/₄ pt/140 ml red vermouth
Salt and pepper as you
  think is needed

Heat the fat contents of the saucepan or roasting tin and stir in the flour – a flat wire whisk (known as a batter whisk) is easiest for this. Let it cook for a minute then, stirring all the time, gradually add the stock, stirring till the gravy boils. Lastly stir in the tomato purée and vermouth. Check the seasoning and add salt and pepper as you think.

Apple and Thyme Sauce

---

2 oz/56 g butter
1 onion, skinned and very
  finely chopped
4 cooking apples, peeled,
  quartered, cored and
  chopped
A good sprig of fresh thyme,
  tiny leaves stripped from

the stalks, or 2 pinches of
dried thyme; I think
thyme is one of two herbs
(the other being
rosemary) which dry
passably well
1 tsp sugar or honey
Salt and pepper

Melt the butter and cook the onion over a moderate heat for several minutes till it is really soft. Then add the chopped apples and cook until they fall into mush, which cooking apples do. Add the thyme and sugar or honey. Taste, and season with salt and pepper if you like. Strange as it may sound, the sautéed onion adds a certain amount of sweetness to this otherwise tart sauce.

Roast Leg of Lamb, with (a) Rosemary and Apple Jelly, (b) Mint Jelly

If I had to choose which roast meat I prefer above all others I think, on balance, it would have to be roast lamb. I love the flavour of lamb, and the vegetables which go so very well with it, like onions or leeks in a creamy white sauce, new peas with finely chopped mint forked through them just before serving, any of the green vegetables – all of these are good with any roast meat but are best of all with lamb. I don't much like mint sauce – too vinegary for my taste, and as such it tends to override the flavours of the meat. But I love herb jellies or redcurrant jelly (best if it's homemade) with roast lamb. And so far I have been talking about roast lamb eaten hot. A leg of lamb roasted in the morning and served at room temperature for dinner or supper the same day is a delicious way to serve a convenient main course. It has none of the congealed fat about it which leftover roast lamb from the previous day has – but I do love that, too.

Same-day roast lamb can be served with hot or cold vegetables – for example, spinach cooked just till it wilts, then dressed with the best olive oil, a brief squeeze of lemon juice and plenty of black pepper, and left to cool before eating. Or any Mediterranean way of cooking vegetables, like cauliflower steamed till just tender, then dressed with olive oil and really good capers. A good ratatouille, or baked aubergines, all these and many more are perfect accompaniments to room temperature roast lamb.

When it comes to roasting the lamb I like flying in the face of fashion because I do not like lamb roasted rare. It is a shame for those who do, because it is safer, too, to cook meat through. Having said that, I don't like lamb roasted till it is positively grey in colour.

To Roast Lamb

I trim off excess fat and rub the leg all over with softened butter. I stick a sharp knife into it in frequent places and stick slivers of garlic in the cuts. I season the leg with salt and plenty of black pepper, and I scatter rosemary over it. I pour about 1 pint/570 ml of red wine over the lamb in its roasting tin and roast it for 20 minutes per pound weight in a very hot oven initially – for the first 45 minutes of cooking at 425°F/220°C/Gas Mark 7, then I reduce the heat a bit, to 400°F/200°C/Gas Mark 6, for the rest of the cooking time. Allow about 20 minutes after the cooking time is up for the lamb to sit in a very low temperature oven before carving, if you are serving it hot – this allows the juices to settle and makes carving much easier. Of course this isn't necessary if you are serving the lamb at room temperature.

Rosemary and Apple Jelly

MAKES 3–4 LB/1.4–1.8 KG

2 lb/900 g apples – windfalls, or eating apples with a good flavour	Several sprigs of rosemary 2 lb/900 g preserving or granulated sugar, more or less depending on the quantity of juice

Wash the apples then chop them in chunks, with peel, core, the lot and put them and the rosemary into a solid and large saucepan with 3 pints/1.7 litres of water. Let them simmer very gently, with the lid on the pan, till the apples are really soft, mushy when pressed against the sides of the pan with your wooden spoon. This can take up to an hour.

Drain the juice of the contents of the pan through a muslin or jelly bag – this is best done overnight. Don't be tempted to squeeze the contents of a muslin or a jelly bag into a bowl because that will give you a cloudy jelly. If possible, leave it to drip and drain overnight. Measure the juice and allow 1 lb/450 g sugar per pint/570 ml of juice. Over a gentle heat, dissolve the sugar in the apple and rosemary liquid, taking great care not to let the liquid reach boiling point till there is no more grittiness under your wooden spoon. Then boil it fast. After 10 minutes' fast boil, draw the pan off the heat, drip some liquid on to a cold saucer and leave the saucer for several minutes. Push the trickle of jelly with your fingertips; if the jelly wrinkles you have a set. If it is still runny, replace the pan on the heat, bring the contents to the boil and boil fast once more. Repeat the testing after a further 5 minutes' boiling, remembering to pull the pan off the heat.

When you have reached setting point, pot the hot jelly into hot jamjars. Seal. When cold, label and store on a shelf in a cool cupboard or larder.

Mint Jelly

This is my favourite jelly for eating with lamb.

MAKES 3–4 LB/1.4–1.8 KG

2 lb/900 g apples, half of them cookers and the rest eating apples	*½ pt/285 ml white wine vinegar*
Several good handfuls of mint, preferably applemint which has the best flavour	*2 lb/900 g preserving or granulated sugar, more or less depending on the quantity of liquid*

Chop the apples – wash them first – and put them into a heavy saucepan with half the mint, 3 pints/1.7 litres of water and the white wine vinegar. Cover the pan with its lid and simmer the contents very gently till the apples are really soft, mushy when pressed against the sides of the pan with your wooden spoon. Strain the liquid through a muslin or jelly bag – this is best done overnight. Don't be tempted to squeeze the contents of the muslin because that will give you a cloudy jelly.

Meanwhile, strip the remaining mint leaves from the stalks and chop them roughly. Measure the strained liquid back into a clean pan, and add 1 lb/450 g sugar for each pint/570 ml of liquid. Over a moderate heat dissolve the sugar in the liquid, taking great care not to let the liquid boil before the sugar is completely dissolved. Then boil it fast. After 10 minutes draw the pan off the heat and trickle some liquid on to a cold saucer. Leave for several minutes, then push the surface with your finger tip – if it wrinkles, you have a set. If not, reboil for a further 5 minutes before testing again. Just before the final test, stir the chopped mint through the liquid.

When you have reached a set, pot into clean jars, and seal, as above.

Roast Beef with (a) Horseradish Cream, (b) Pink Peppercorn Sauce

Beef is one meat that I do like to eat cooked rare, but not so rare that it is bleeding on the plate, as two members of our family like it. Which cut of beef you roast depends on your taste – and the depth of your purse. I would choose a rib roast every time, and on the bone. I very much prefer to roast all meats on the bone, both for added flavour and to prevent shrinkage. I do know that some people roast silverside, but I think that it is too dry a cut to roast successfully and it is much better braised. I roast beef for 10–15 minutes per pound with 10 minutes over at 425°F/220°C/Gas Mark 7. This seems to satisfy all of the varying tastes in our family – the bloodiest centre is perfect for Godfrey and Meriel, whereas the rest of us prefer the rather less undercooked bits.

I have to admit here and now to a complete inability to make Yorkshire pudding. Coming as I do from nearby Lancashire, there is really no excuse. I have followed the recipes of a variety of reputable cooks to the letter, leaving the batter to stand, and I invariably end up with the same disappointing result, puddingy of texture with not a crispness anywhere to my poor puddings. I have made them so often, individually, or in large roasting tins as my mother makes them, and I just can't understand why they are always a dismal failure for me – very bad for the morale, but at least I'm honest! Peter, who cooks here with me, makes the most perfect Yorkshire pud, so when we have roast beef I ask him very nicely if he will make the Yorkshire pudding. You can, I have been told, buy very good Yorkshire puddings in Marks & Spencer, to my utter amazement, but I haven't – yet – tried them.

As with all roast meats, leave the piece of cooked beef to stand for 15 minutes in a very low temperature oven to let the juices settle, which makes carving easier.

Horseradish Cream

You can buy a wide variety of horseradish sauces and relishes, but if you can, buy a jar of grated horseradish. It isn't easy to find, but you do occasionally come across them in good delicatessens. Or buy it fresh, peel it and grate it – beware, it is ferociously fiery in its raw state, so use it sparingly. Mix it with whipped cream or, better still, with crème fraîche.

Pink Peppercorn Sauce

This is so simple and so good with roast beef – or with steaks.

FOR 6

Half a jar of pink peppercorns, drained of their brine	*1 tub of crème fraîche (7 fl oz/200 ml)*

Mix together the pink peppercorns and crème fraîche, and serve in a bowl to accompany the roast beef.

Roast Chicken with Creamy Saffron and Lemon Sauce

Straight roast chicken is the favourite of just about everyone, providing, that is, that the chicken is really good, as free-range as is possible to procure where you live. Straight roast chicken needs bread sauce as its accompaniment, and possibly rolls of bacon too, if we are being strictly correct. But I don't much like rolls of bacon, because I don't like the way that the bacon inside the roll doesn't crisp up – it can't. So for my taste, and very luckily for the tastes of all seven of our immediate family, I like to make this simple sauce to accompany roast chicken – simple it is, but indulgent in its components. The saffron and lemon and cream all complement each other and the chicken.

SERVES 4

1 chicken weighing about 3 lb/1.4 kg	*½ pt/285 ml good chicken stock*
1 lemon, cut in half	*2 good pinches of saffron strands*
About 2 oz/56 g softened butter	*Juice of 1 lemon + grated rind of 1 lemon*
Salt and black pepper	*½ pt/285 ml double cream*
For the sauce:	*Salt and freshly ground black pepper*
2 oz/56 g butter	
1 onion, skinned and very finely chopped	

Put the chicken into a roasting tin with the lemon halves inside it. Rub it with softened butter and season it with salt and pepper. Roast in a hot oven, 425°F/200°C/Gas Mark 7, for 20 minutes, then reduce the heat to 400°F/200°C/Gas Mark 6 for a further 25 minutes, or so – till when you stick the point of a knife into the bit between the leg and the body the juices run clear. Leave the chicken in a low temperature oven, once cooked, for 10 minutes, to let the juices settle.

Make the sauce by melting the butter in a sauté pan and cooking the very finely chopped onion over moderate heat till it is really soft. Add the chicken stock and saffron and simmer till the stock has reduced by more than half. Add the lemon rind and juice and reduce for a further couple of minutes' cooking. Pour in the cream –

it must be double, the danger with single cream is that it can curdle, or split. Double won't. Let the sauce bubble till it has the texture of thick cream. Season with salt and pepper.

Serve in a bowl to accompany the sliced roast chicken. The sauce will be a golden colour, from the saffron – don't be tempted to substitute saffron powder, which is generally adulterated, only the strands will do!

Roast Venison with Port and Redcurrant Jelly Gravy

I am sure that some people are put off eating venison because they imagine it to have a strong and gamey flavour, which it doesn't. Venison is a most useful meat, and widely available to us now in supermarkets' butchery departments and in butchers' shops as well as poulterers and from game dealers. Venison is a red meat but a very unfatty meat, and this can present a problem when it is cooked as it tends to be a dry meat. If you roast venison in the following way you should avoid dryness. Beware of overcooking.

SERVES 6–8

About 3 oz/84 g softened butter or beef dripping
2 onions, skinned and chopped
2 leeks, trimmed and sliced
1 parsnip and 1 carrot, each peeled and chopped
½ lb/285 g mushrooms, wiped and chopped
A piece of venison, preferably cut from the

haunch, weighing about 7–8 lb/3–3.5 kg (venison shrinks more than any other meat I can think of)
½ pt/285 ml port + ½ pt/ 285 ml water
Salt and pepper
2 tsp redcurrant jelly
1 pt/570 ml vegetable or beef stock

Melt the butter or dripping in the roasting pan and sauté the chopped onions over moderate heat till they are golden brown. Add the sliced leeks and the rest of the vegetables and cook them with the sautéed onions till they are all soft – about 5 minutes. Put the venison on the vegetables and spoon some vegetables on the top. Pour in the port and water and season with salt and pepper. Roast in a hot oven, 425°F/220°C/Gas Mark 7, for 30 minutes, then take the tin out of the oven and cover it closely with foil, tucking the foil under the edge of the roasting tin. Put it back in the oven but at a moderate temperature – 350°F/180°C/Gas Mark 4 – for 2 hours for an 8 lb/3.5 kg piece of meat. Before serving, let the meat sit in a low temperature oven to let the juices settle.

Put the contents of the tin, apart from the meat itself, into a food processor or liquidizer, add the redcurrant jelly, and whiz the contents till smooth, adding stock (or port, if you prefer) till it is the consistency you like as some prefer a much thinner gravy and some a thicker gravy. It does depend on individual preference just how much of the stock you add. Pour the gravy into a saucepan and reheat gently before serving with the carved venison.

Roast Rack of Lamb with a Herb Crust

I have seen – and bought – racks of lamb for sale in butchers' departments of supermarkets and they are so convenient, especially when you are only a few for lunch. They cook so much more quickly than a large leg of lamb. How long you roast it depends on how pink you like to eat your lamb. Do trim as much fat as possible off each rack, because it doesn't get a chance to crisp up under the herb crust. I like to serve this with a sauced vegetable, like leeks in a nutmeg-flavoured creamy white sauce, and with crispy sautéed potatoes with paprika.

Allow 2–3 chops per person, depending on their ages and therefore, to a great extent, their appetites.

2 oz/56 g butter + 2 tbsp olive oil	*cut off the crusts before whizzing the bread to crumbs*
1 onion, chopped as finely and neatly as possible	*Salt and pepper*
1 clove of garlic, skinned and very finely chopped	*2 tbsp finely chopped parsley, snipped chives and chopped tarragon*
6 oz/170 g day-old breadcrumbs made from baked bread, as opposed to steamed sliced bread;	*2 racks of lamb each with 6–7 chops in it*

Melt the butter and heat the oil together and sauté the onion in this till it is really soft – about 5 minutes. Stir in the garlic, cook for a minute, then stir in the breadcrumbs, salt and pepper, off the heat, and lastly the chopped herbs. Mix all together very well. Trim all the fat you can from the racks. Lay them so the fat side is uppermost, flat. Spoon over the herb crust, pressing it down well, and roast in a hot oven, 400°F/200°C/Gas Mark 6, for 25 minutes – 30 minutes if you prefer slightly better-cooked lamb.

Roast Duck with Apple Cream Gravy

So many people love duck that I can't think why you don't find it eaten more often in homes. It is thought of far more as a restaurant food. It's so easy, I mean, all you need is a really sharp pair of game shears to cut the duck in quarters. But how I loathe undercooked duck. Duck flesh should be cooked through without being shredded, and the skin should be crisp – utterly delicious. What is to me quite repellent is duck, whole or just duck breasts, undercooked with that layer of fat just under the surface of the skin. Can anyone seriously enjoy their duck like this? I can't think so. It's just a case of people not daring to admit it!

The best domestic ducks are, to my mind, Gressingham ducks. They are so aptly named, because in the village of Gressingham, very near my parents' home in North Lancashire, there is an exquisite small house set in a most lovingly laid out and cared-for garden. Until her far too early death last year, Mrs Hogg lived in this house and cooked duck to perfection for guests to her house. She started running her home as a most exclusive small restaurant when my grandmother was alive, and she died over thirty years ago, but all that time Mr and Mrs Hogg were friends of ours. Latterly, in the last fifteen or more years, you had to plan so far ahead that a table reservation was needed months and months in advance. Apart from the elegant surroundings, the lure was Mrs Hogg's roast duck. She always cooked roast duck for the main course, and people came from far and wide to eat her roast duck. My father once tried to calculate how many ducks must have passed through Mrs Hogg's kitchen but he had to give up counting! There was no nonsense about undercooking duck there, and that was why her roast duck was legendary. Mrs Hogg could be formidable, but she was a wonderful person, and so is Colin, her husband.

Duck is a great favourite both on the menu here at Kinloch and for a special occasion lunch party. For eight people, allow two ducks. If you are only six, cold roast duck is delicious eaten up the next day.

Put the ducks in a roasting tin in a hot oven, 425°F/220°C/Gas Mark 7, and roast them for 1 hour and about 10 minutes.

Apple and Cream Gravy

The creamy content of this gravy is actually crème fraîche, which is less rich – slightly! – than cream, and which has the right acidic kick to sharpen up the sauce to complement the rich roast duck meat.

2 oz/56 g butter	1 tsp flour
1 onion, skinned and very finely chopped	1/2 pt/285 ml dry cider – as dry as you can get
3 good eating apples – Cox's would be ideal – skinned, cored and chopped as finely as possible	1/2 pt/285 ml crème fraîche
	Salt and freshly ground black pepper

Melt the butter in a sauté pan and gently sauté the chopped onion till it is really soft, about 5 minutes. Then add the chopped apples to the sauté pan, stir in the flour and pour in the cider. Simmer till the cider has reduced by about half. Stir in the crème fraîche, and season with salt and pepper. Let the sauce bubble for a few minutes. Keep the sauce warm till you are able to serve it with the duck.

To serve the duck, cut each in half with a very good pair of scissors or, better still, game shears. Trim off the legs at the tops and cut down either side of the backbone for a neater appearance.

Steamed Leeks in White Sauce

I think that any vegetable in a creamy well-made white sauce makes a good vegetable accompaniment to a roast meat, but leeks in white sauce are especially good with Roast Leg of Lamb and with Roast Rack of Lamb with a Herb Crust. They are also delicious with Steak, Kidney and Mushroom Pie, and with Game Pudding, too. It is so much better to steam the leeks rather than to simmer them in water, because, like onions, leeks hold so much water that when they are cooked in it, it is pretty well impossible to drain them. The water seeps out from between the layered leaves of leek and makes the sauce watery. By steaming them you avoid direct water contact with the leeks.

6 good medium-sized leeks, each trimmed and washed well and sliced on the diagonal – it looks nicer – about 2 inches/5 cm thick	*2 oz/56 g butter* *2 oz/56 g flour* *1 pt/570 ml milk* *Salt and freshly ground black pepper* *A grating of whole nutmeg*

Steam the leeks till you can stick a fork in them and they feel tender.

Melt the butter and stir in the flour. Let it cook for a minute before stirring in the milk, gradually, adding a small amount at a time. You may find a wire whisk better than a wooden spoon for this. Stir till the sauce reaches simmering point. Let it simmer gently for a minute, then draw the pan off the heat and season with salt, pepper and nutmeg.

Put the cooked leeks into a warmed ovenproof dish and pour the sauce over them. Gently, so as not to break them up, stir the sauce into the leeks. Cover closely to prevent a skin forming if you want to keep the leeks in white sauce warm, which they do very successfully without spoiling. You can actually prepare them the day before and reheat them gently, stirring them occasionally, and my sister has even frozen leeks in white sauce.

Sautéed Onions in White Sauce

Onion sauce is a classic accompaniment for roast lamb, but I much prefer to enlarge the sauce into vegetable status. I don't like to boil the onions – like leeks, onions hold so much water within their layers that they are difficult to drain, resulting in a diluted white sauce. I also find that steaming onions, unless they are very small onions, is a very lengthy process. The result is that for onions in white sauce I sauté them gently in a thick-based pan with the lid on. I pay frequent attention to them, shaking the pan from time to time and checking that the onions within aren't browning too much. Stick a fork into the largest onion, or, if you have cut them in quarters, the largest piece of onion. When it is tender they are cooked.

Like the leeks, Sautéed Onions in White Sauce reheats well, and it, too, can be frozen. The sauce, on thawing, looks horribly separated but don't worry, as it reheats it all comes together satisfactorily.

SERVES 6

2 oz/56 g butter + 1 tbsp	*quarter them*
sunflower oil, or dripping	For the sauce:
from the roast lamb tin	*2 oz/56 g butter*
2 lb/900 g onions, skinned	*2 oz/56 g flour*
and cut in quarters, or	*1 pt/570 ml milk*
left whole, depending	*Salt and pepper*
which you prefer – I	*Freshly grated nutmeg*

In a large heavy sauté pan, preferably non-stick (the best are made by a German firm called Wol), melt the butter and heat the oil or dripping together. Over gentle to moderate heat cook the onions, shaking the pan till they are soft – this is speedier if you cover the pan with a lid, but do watch the contents, so as not to burn them.

Melt the butter in a saucepan and stir in the flour. Let this cook for a minute and then gradually add the milk, stirring all the time till the sauce boils. You may find this easier to do with a wire whisk, called a 'batter' whisk – an invaluable piece of kitchen equipment. Let the sauce simmer briefly, then take the pan off the heat and season to your taste with salt, pepper and nutmeg.

Stir the cooked onions into the sauce and pour into a warm serving dish. Cover closely and keep the dish warm till you are ready to serve.

Braised Cabbage with Nutmeg

Cabbage, however you cook it, goes so very well with any type of meat or chicken or duck. Braised, the cabbage is easier to cook and to keep warm without spoiling.

You will, perhaps, notice that nutmeg is used to season all these vegetable dishes. I think that nutmeg is the most versatile of all spices, complementing as it does such a wide range of foods, from vegetables to cheese, fish to meat, and soft fruits and cream- and milk-based puddings. It doesn't matter what meat you intend this cabbage to accompany, I tend to cook it in chicken stock. You can use vegetable stock if you prefer.

SERVES 6

---

2 oz/56 g butter + 1 tbsp either sunflower or olive oil

1 medium-sized white cabbage, or 2 medium savoys, trimmed of outer leaves and tough stalks,

and shredded as finely as possible

1 pt/570 ml chicken or vegetable stock

Salt and freshly ground pepper

Freshly grated nutmeg

Melt the butter and heat the oil, and stir-fry the cabbage in this till it is all turned in the butter/oil. Pour in the stock, bring it to simmering point, season with salt, pepper and nutmeg, and simmer very gently, stirring occasionally, till the largest bit is tender when stuck with a fork. As it simmers, the stock will reduce. I find the best type of pan to use to cook this is a wide sauté pan – that way the cabbage cooks evenly and the stock reduces.

To keep the cabbage warm cover it, in a warmed serving dish, and keep it in a low temperature oven.

Braised Celery

You do have to be careful with celery – it falls into the category of foods which people love or loathe. It goes so well, though, with all manner of meats, and chicken and duck, that if you are sure of the taste of your guests it is a delicious and convenient vegetable. As it is a rather nondescript vegetable dish from an appearance point of view, it is as well to have something with a splash of colour as another vegetable – like puréed turnip or swedes for example, or carrots sliced into julienne strips and stir-fried with lemon, and with chopped parsley stirred through just before serving.

Serves 6

2 good heads of celery	*combination is*
2 oz/56 g butter	*particularly good if the*
1 pt/570 ml stock, or ½ pt/	*celery is to go with*
285 ml stock + ½ pt/285	*chicken*
ml dry white wine – this	Salt, pepper and nutmeg

Trim the stalk end off the celery, and cut away any outer stalks. Chop off most of the leaves – keep them for stock – but leave some. Strip off any stringy bits. Slice into diagonal bits about 1 inch/2.5 cm long. Melt the butter in a wide heavy sauté pan and cook the celery in the butter for a couple of minutes, stirring so that each bit of celery is coated. Pour in the stock and season with salt, pepper and nutmeg.

Simmer very gently till the stock reduces and the celery is soft when stuck with a fork. In a warmed dish, closely covered, this celery keeps warm very successfully without spoiling.

Purée of Garden Peas with Applemint

The nicest way to eat peas is when they are tiny and need the briefest cooking time, and are mixed with butter and chopped mint.

But all too often peas are picked too big, and their flavour alters a bit – not for the better – and their texture is coarse and can veer towards the cardboard by description. Then, given peas in this state (and the test is when you eat some raw whether they taste sweet to you or not), by puréeing them with applemint you can transform them into a vegetable dish which is delicious.

Peas like this go well with any roast meat or chicken or duck. The other thing to bear in mind is not to cook the mint in with the peas. Mint, like many other herbs (the exceptions being rosemary and thyme), loses most of its flavour when in heat for any length of time. The small amount of white sauce is necessary; it acts as a 'binder' to the pea purée.

SERVES 6

1½ lb/675 g peas	*A grating of nutmeg*
1 oz/28 g butter	*About a handful of mint*
1 oz/28 g flour	*leaves, preferably*
½ pt/285 ml creamy milk	*applemint, stripped from*
Salt and pepper	*the stalks*

Steam or simmer the peas till tender. Drain and rinse briefly under cold water, which refreshes their colour.

Meanwhile, melt the butter and stir in the flour. Let this cook for a moment then, stirring all the time, gradually stir (or whisk) in the milk, stirring till the sauce bubbles. Take the pan off the heat and season with salt and pepper, and nutmeg. Cover the surface with a butter paper, to prevent a skin forming.

Whiz the peas and sauce with the mint leaves. Taste, and season if you think it needs more salt and pepper. Reheat gently, or just put this mixture into a buttered warmed serving dish, and serve.

Vegetable Pie with Lemon Grass and a Crisp Crust

This is a delicious dish, intended for those who don't eat meat. But it has been very much enjoyed by many who love meat, yet are happy to have a meal without meat as its main part. Lemon grass is easily available these days, although not yet to be found on the shelves of the Co-op in Broadford, my local food mecca. Judging by the food items we can buy now that I would never have thought to even look for in Skye, within the next year or so I expect I shall even be able to buy lemon grass in our local Co-op. But if you too live in an out-of-the-way spot like I do, then feel safe in buying lemon grass a couple of weeks before you use it – it keeps very well in the fridge. You need to snap a stick in half to release its flavour.

SERVES 6

*4 carrots, peeled and cut
into chunks*
1 pt/570 ml creamy milk
*1 stick of lemon grass,
broken in half*
*2 oz/56 g butter + 2 tbsp
sunflower or olive oil*
*4 sticks celery, wiped and
trimmed and sliced finely*
*1 onion, skinned and finely
chopped*
*4 leeks, washed well and
trimmed and sliced in
1-inch/2.5 cm bits*
4 average-sized courgettes,

*wiped and ends cut off,
and cut into chunks*
*½ lb/225 g mushrooms,
wiped and sliced*
1½ tbsp (just rounded) flour
*Salt and plenty of freshly
ground pepper*
For the topping:
2 oz/56 g butter, melted
*1 clove of garlic, skinned
and very finely chopped*
*6 oz/170 g brown
breadcrumbs – we use the
granary bread we make
each day for crumbs*
3 oz/84 g flaked almonds

Steam the carrot chunks till you can stick a fork into the largest bit and it feels tender. Put the creamy milk (or single cream) into a saucepan with the broken lemon grass stick and heat gently over a moderate heat till a skin forms. Take the pan off the heat and leave to cool – the lemon grass will infuse the cream or milk with its flavour.

Melt the butter and add the oil and cook the sliced celery and chopped onion and sliced leeks together for several minutes, stirring from time to time. Sauté these vegetables till they are really soft. Depending on the diameter of the pan you use this will take anything from 5 to 10 minutes. With a slotted spoon scoop them out of the pan on to a dish. Cook the chopped courgettes till they, too, are tender. Scoop them in with the onion, celery and leeks. You may need to add a bit more oil at this point. Raise the heat and sauté the sliced mushrooms till they are very well cooked – almost crisp; this greatly improves their flavour. Stir in the flour. Let it cook for a minute then gradually stir in the flavoured milk or cream (having thrown out the lemon grass), stirring till the mushroomy sauce simmers. Stir in the steamed carrots and the rest of the vegetables. Season to your taste with salt and pepper. Pour into a pie dish.

To make the topping, melt the butter in a saucepan and stir in the chopped garlic, breadcrumbs and flaked almonds. Mix well. Then sprinkle this over the vegetables in the sauce. Bake in a moderate oven, 350°F/180°C/Gas Mark 4, for 30–35 minutes. The top should be crisp and golden brown.

Packed and Picnic Lunches, and Food for the Great Outdoors

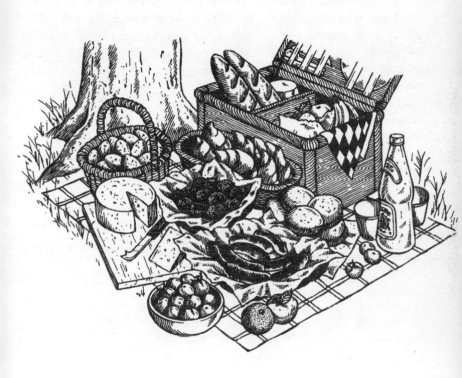

Quails' Scotch Eggs in Sesame Seeds

Frittata with (a) Spinach and Goats' Cheese, (b) Red Onions and Peppers

Bacon, Egg and Lettuce Buns

Crab, Lime Mayonnaise and Cucumber Buns

Anchovy Buttered Buns with Egg Filling

Chicken and Smoked Bacon Filo Parcels

Game Pasty

Apple and Pork Sausagemeat Puffed Roll

Ham Terrine with Quails' Eggs

Pitta Bread with Grainy Mustard and Fillet of Beef

Pitta Bread with Chicken and Roast Red Pepper Mayonnaise

Beef and Tomato Casserole

Jugged Hare with Forcemeat Balls

Venison Pasty

Sausage Hot Pot

Irish Stew with Black Pudding

Beef Stew with Root Vegetables and Mustard Dumplings

Cottage Pie with Julienne Vegetables on top

*Venison (or Pork) Sausages with Braised Red Cabbage and Baked Jacket
Potatoes*

Thick Venison and Vegetable Soup

PACKED AND PICNIC LUNCHES, AND FOOD FOR THE GREAT OUTDOORS

Some of my happiest childhood memories involve picnics. It seems that when I was a child, every day of all the summer holidays was sunny, because I remember – whether accurately or not – daily picnic teas by various rivers, all involving pre-tea swims, or river or beck damming, a pastime I love still. But whether tea, lunch or supper, picnic food, or food eaten out doors, somehow tastes better than any food eaten inside. The smallest amount of food can be classified as a picnic, thereby imbuing a small walk with a young child with an aura of adventure. Alexandra, our eldest daughter, remembers walks with my mother, her beloved Granny, and tiny picnics consisting of raisins and an apple.

But that, fun though it is, is just giving a walk more importance by including something to eat, whereas so many picnics these days are eaten not only for the fun of the excursion (perhaps a lunch-time barbecue on a beach, a great favourite of ours and one always undertaken at least once during the Christmas and New Year holidays), but also because a sport or event lasts all day and food will be required during the day. Such an event can be sheep dog trials, a school sports day, a day's shooting, when the food must do double duty to not only feed those consuming it but also, as often as not, to warm them too. Such food can be transported in wide-necked Thermos flasks – recipes such as the Sausage Hot Pot or the Thick Venison and Vegetable Soup fall into this category, whereas other dishes, such as the Cottage Pie with its unusual vegetable top or the Beef Stew with Root Vegetables and Mustard Dumplings can be easily transported and will hold their heat well provided that the dish they are in is well covered with foil – if you like you can put the dish in a large solid cardboard box, well lined with newspapers, to give further insulation.

Food which doesn't require a knife and fork needn't be restricted to sandwiches, although personally I love a good sandwich. A panic picnic can be so easily collected, provided you have access to a Marks & Spencer where quite the best sandwiches are to be bought! But the alternatives to bread for a picnic are many and varied. The Game Pasty, for example, makes a very good and sustaining picnic main course. So does the Ham Terrine. One of my favourites is a Frittata, and in this chapter are two flavourings, one for a Frittata made with Spinach and Goats' Cheese, the other for a Frittata with well sautéed Red Onions and Peppers, both delicious. There are several suggestions for fillings for good soft buns, such as the egg fillings, and I love the spicy fillet of beef in the pitta-bread, or, if you prefer, the spicy chicken alternative filling for pitta bread.

Whatever type of picnic you plan, you can take the rest of the picnic food to fit in. Good potato crisps are a valuable accessory whatever the occasion, as are cherry tomatoes and bags or a bowl of crisp assorted lettuce leaves. For a completely informal family picnic rolls of kitchen paper are fine, but for anything tidier good thick paper napkins are essential. A cold box with a couple of drinks is vital for warm summer picnics, say, white wine with – my favourite this summer – M & S pink grapefruit juice, and sparking mineral water which can dilute either the wine into spritzers, or the pink grapefruit juice into a long cool drink. A couple of large plastic bags are fairly essential, too, for taking home dirty cutlery and dirty plates. Sadly, there is nothing I can suggest to make the awful clearing up of a picnic any better, but just console yourself with the thought of the next one!

Quails' Scotch Eggs in Sesame Seeds

These make ideal food, being rather less hauntingly hefty than the more usual Scotch egg, made with hens' eggs. As with anything made with sausages, I think it is of paramount importance to use the best sausages you can find – I have yet to find sausagemeat good enough outside of sausage casings. I look for the highest percentage of meat – as opposed to pork, which can include parts of the animal

I wouldn't want to eat whole, like lips and eyelids to name a couple of the more mentionable parts.

12 quails' eggs	*4 oz/112 g sesame seeds*
1 lb/450 g best quality pork	*mixed with ¹/₂ tsp salt*
sausages	*Sunflower oil for frying*

Cook the quails' eggs in simmering water for 3 minutes, then run cold water into the saucepan till the eggs feel cold. Shell them carefully – they have surprisingly hard shells compared to hens' eggs.

Slit each sausage, skin with a sharp knife and peel off the skins. Divide each sausage in half and press out the sausagemeat. Wrap it around a shelled egg, pinching the meat together at the join. Press each sausage-encased egg around in the sesame seeds.

Shallow fry in a preferably non-stick frying pan, in a small amount of sunflower oil, turning the eggs over – I use two forks for this – till they are golden brown all over. As they cook, remove them to a plate lined with kitchen paper, to absorb excess oil. Pack them for the picnic either whole or cut in half, whichever you prefer.

Frittata

A frittata is a thick Italian omelette, served at room temperature. It is ideal picnic food, because you can vary the flavourings to suit your tastes, it is easy to transport, and it only needs to be cut into wedges to serve. You can make it a day ahead, but it is much nicer made in the morning for a picnic lunch.

Frittata with Spinach and Goats' Cheese

Don't be tempted to make this in a crêpe or omelette pan wider than 8 inches/20 cm, because the frittata should be about 1 inch/2.5 cm deep, rather than a thinner and therefore more leathery textured cold omelette!

MAKES 6 WEDGES

6 large eggs	*2 oz/56 g baby spinach, torn*
Salt and plenty of freshly	*into bits*
ground black pepper	*3 oz/84 g soft goats' cheese,*
1 tbsp olive oil + 1 oz/28 g	*crumbled into bits*
butter	

Beat the eggs together well, seasoning them with salt and pepper. Heat the oil and butter in an omelette or crêpe pan 8 inches/20 cm diameter and, when the oil and melted butter are hot, pour in the egg mixture, adding the torn-up spinach and crumbled cheese, and stirring around the contents of the pan for a few seconds. Then stop stirring and leave the pan on a very low heat indeed, for about 10 minutes. The contents will be firm but the top will still be runny. Heat a grill, but not too full on red-hot heat, just turn it on halfway and set the frittata – but do watch out not to brown it, or it will toughen.

When it is firm and set, slip the frittata from the pan onto several thicknesses of kitchen paper to cool. Wrap in foil for the picnic, having first cut the frittata into six wedges.

Frittata with Red Onions and Peppers

This frittata needs a little more preparation in that the peppers, for maximum enjoyment, should be skinned, and the onions and skinned peppers are then gently sautéed together till the onions are really soft. Add as much garlic as you like.

MAKES 6 WEDGES

3 red (or yellow) peppers	*1 tbsp olive oil + 1 oz/28 g*
2 tbsp olive oil for cooking	*butter for cooking the*
the onions and pepper	*frittata*
2 red onions, skinned and	*6 large eggs*
finely chopped	*Salt and plenty of freshly*
2 cloves of garlic, skinned	*ground black pepper*
and chopped finely	

Start by cutting the peppers in half, removing the seeds, and grilling under a red-hot grill till the peppers form great charred blisters. Then put the pepper halves into a polythene bag and leave for 10 minutes. The skins should then peel off easily. Chop the skinned peppers quite small.

Heat the 2 tablespoons of olive oil in a sauté pan and sauté the chopped red onions for 5 minutes over a moderate to gentle heat. Then stir in the chopped garlic and chopped peppers and continue to cook for a further 5 minutes. Let this mixture cool.

Heat the tablespoon of olive oil with the butter in a crêpe or omelette pan 8 inches/20 cm in diameter. Beat the eggs, seasoning them with salt and pepper, and, when the oil and melted butter are hot, pour in the eggs, mixing in the onion, garlic and pepper mixture, and stirring all together for a few seconds. The turn the heat under the pan right down low, and leave the frittata to cook, without any more stirring, for 10 minutes. It should be firm, but still runny on top.

Heat the grill to halfway heat – not red-hot by any means – and gently cook the top of the frittata under the grill, just till the top is firm – but not browned, which makes the frittata leathery in texture.

Slip the cooked frittata onto several thicknesses of kitchen paper to cool. When cold, cut into six wedges and wrap in foil.

Bacon, Egg and Lettuce Buns

These are the buns I make for a picnic when I am stuck for an idea, because I know that they are the family favourite. It is generally recognized within our family that my mother makes the best egg and bacon buns – she is a dab hand at many other things besides – but these come a close second to hers. Good buns are essential, and I split them open – easiest with a serrated knife – trying to leave them joined at one section, and carefully pull out the dough from the top and bottom of each bun, to make room for more filling which, because of the cavity created by the dough removal, then hopefully won't squidge out of the bun on biting.

How many you allow per person depends entirely on the age and appetite (the two are directly connected) of the guests.

FILLS 6 BUNS

8 large eggs, hardboiled by simmering them for 5 minutes, then running cold water into the saucepan till the eggs are cold

4 oz/112 g softened butter

4 tbsp mayonnaise – preferably homemade

1 tsp mustard powder (or Dijon mustard, if you prefer)

A pinch of salt – the bacon will add saltiness – and lots of pepper

8 rashers smoked streaky bacon, grilled till crisp then broken, into small bits

Crisp lettuce leaves

Prepare the buns as described in the introduction. Shell the eggs and put them into a deep bowl. With a sharp knife cut the eggs till they are chopped as fine as you like – I find it less messy to cut them in the bowl rather than chop them on a board – and then mash in the softened butter, mayonnaise, mustard powder, salt and pepper. Mash and mix all together well. Lastly, mix in the broken bits of bacon.

Line each bun with lettuce on one half, and divide the egg and bacon mixture between the buns. Slice each in half with a serrated knife, for easier eating, and wrap in clingfilm.

Crab, Lime Mayonnaise and Cucumber Buns

This is a filling for buns for a special occasion. The type of bun you choose to encase this filling is dependent on your preference – either soft white baps or crisper-crusted granary rolls. But as the filling tends to be rather moist, I suggest the buns are split and buttered and the filling taken separately, in a bowl, with a spoon to fill each bun before eating. It takes a matter of seconds to fill the buns.

FILLS 6 LARGE BUNS

---

1 egg + 1 yolk
1 tsp caster sugar
1/2 tsp salt and plenty of freshly ground black pepper
Grated rind of 1 lime
1/3 pt/190 ml mixed olive and sunflower oils

Juice of 2 limes
Half a cucumber
1 lb/450 g crabmeat; I prefer half white and half brown meat, mixed – I think the brown meat has more flavour

---

To make the mayonnaise, put the egg, yolk, sugar, salt, pepper and lime rind into a processor and whiz, gradually adding the oils – drop by drop initially, then, when you have an emulsion, in a thin trickle. Lastly, whiz in the lime juice. Adjust the seasoning by adding more salt and pepper if you like.

Peel the cucumber with a potato peeler and cut the flesh into chunks. Cut each chunk in half and scoop out the seeds, then dice the flesh. This prevents the cucumber making the filling watery.

Mix together the crabmeat, mayonnaise and diced cucumber.

Put this into a Pyrex bowl (so much easier to wash afterwards than a solid plastic bowl) and store in the fridge till the moment of departure. Transport the crab filling in a cold box.

Anchovy Buttered Buns with Egg Filling

The flavours of egg and anchovy combine together so well. The anchovy gives the eggy taste an interesting kick, but it is essential to make the egg mixture creamy in taste and texture. You achieve this by mixing the chopped hardboiled eggs with softened butter and good mayonnaise. For this I prefer brown wholemeal or granary buns.

FILLS 6 BUNS

8 large eggs	*Plenty of black pepper – no*
Butter for the buns	*need for salt, because the*
Patum peperium, anchovy	*anchovy paste is salty*
paste	*enough for most people*
2 oz/56 g softened butter	*Crisp lettuce leaves (Cos or*
4 tbsp good mayonnaise	*Iceberg)*

Boil the eggs for 5 minutes, then run cold water into the saucepan to cool them quickly and prevent them continuing to cook in the hot water after you take the saucepan off the heat. Shell them and chop them, with a knife, in a bowl.

Scoop out the central dough from each bun, after slicing them nearly in half – leave the halves joined by about 2 inches/5 cm. Butter both halves of each bun and spread them as liberally or sparingly as you choose with patum peperium.

Mix the chopped eggs with the softened butter, mayonnaise and pepper. Lay a lettuce leaf on each bun and divide the egg filling between them.

Gently press down the buttered top of each bun, wrap them in clingfilm, and store them in a cool place till you are ready to transport your picnic. How many buns you allow per person depends entirely on the age and, therefore, appetite of the person.

Chicken and Smoked Bacon Filo Parcels

Apart from bread, pastry of whichever sort, puff, short, or as in this case filo, is an excellent way to encase a substantial filling for a picnic. The smoked bacon in the filling for these filo parcels is delicious and adds a complementary flavour to the chicken.

Allow 3–4 parcels per person, depending on age (which is an indication of appetite) and whether this is the main part of the picnic or one of two or three items.

MAKES 16 PARCELS ABOUT 3 INCHES/7.5 CM SQUARE

2 tbsp either sunflower or olive oil	*4 cooked chicken breasts (either roast or poached), skin removed, the chicken meat cut into fine dice*
1 onion, skinned and finely chopped	
6 rashers of the best smoked back bacon, sliced into fine dice – easy with a really sharp knife	*A pinch – no more – of salt and plenty of freshly ground black pepper*
8 oz/225 g cream cheese such as Philadelphia	*8 sheets of filo pastry*
	Melted butter in a saucepan

Heat the oil in a saucepan or frying pan and cook the finely chopped onion and bacon together, stirring, till the onion is soft and beginning to turn golden, and the bacon is well cooked. Cool this mixture. In a bowl beat the cream cheese till it is smooth and creamy (you can do this in a food processor but then scrape it into a bowl), and mix in the finely diced chicken meat, the seasoning, and the cooled onion and bacon mixture.

Lay a sheet of filo on a table or work surface and brush

completely with melted butter, using a pastry brush. Cover with a second sheet of filo, and brush again with melted butter. Cut the double sheets in half widthways, then in half across. Put a spoonful of filling in the centre of each square and fold the edges inwards, to form a parcel. Brush each parcel with melted butter and put them on a butter-brushed baking tray.

You can do all this in advance, if you keep the parcels, covered with clingfilm, in a cool place till you are ready to bake them. To cook them, bake in a hot oven, 425°F/220°C/Gas Mark 7, for 7–10 minutes, or till the pastry is golden and crisp. Cool them a bit before wrapping them in baking parchment, then in foil, to transport them. If you wrap them when they are too hot the danger is that they will become soggy. Failing the baking parchment, you can wrap them in a teatowel and then in foil.

Game Pasty

These are convenient in that they can be made in advance – you can make the game filling well ahead and freeze it, if that is going to save you time, thawing it to fill and cook the pasties. If you like you can use puff pastry for these, but I prefer shortcrust pastry.

MAKES 8 PASTIES

1 lb/450 g game meat cut from whatever bird (or venison) you have	1 clove of garlic (optional), skinned and chopped finely
2–3 tbsp sunflower or olive oil	1 level tbsp flour
1 onion, skinned and finely chopped	¾ pt/420 ml game or beef stock
2 carrots, peeled and finely diced	1 tbsp tomato purée
1 leek, washed, trimmed and diced	2 tsp redcurrant jelly
	Salt and pepper
	1½ lb/675 g shortcrust pastry

Briefly whiz the raw game meat in a food processor, but be careful not to pulverize it; it should have the texture of coarsely minced meat. Heat the oil in a heavy sauté pan and cook the game meat till it is well browned. With a slotted spoon scoop it out, draining off excess oil, and put it into a warm dish.

Lower the heat a bit under the sauté pan and cook together the onion, carrots, leek and garlic, stirring them around and cooking for about 5 minutes. Then stir in the flour, let it cook for a minute, then stir in the stock, tomato purée and redcurrant jelly. Season with salt and pepper, replace the browned game meat and stir it in well. Cover with a lid and cook in a moderate oven (remove the handle of the sauté pan first), 350°F/180°C/Gas Mark 4 for 30 minutes. Then cool.

To assemble the pasties, roll out the pastry and cut into eight circles each about 6 inches/15 cm in diameter. Put a spoonful of the game mixture in the middle of each circle of pastry, pushing it to an oblong shape. Dampen the edges with milk, pinch them together to form a pasty shape (like traditional Cornish pasties), and put them on a baking tray. Lightly oil the baking tray if it doesn't have a non-stick surface. Bake in a hot oven, 425°F/220°C/Gas Mark 7, for 15–20 minutes, till the pastry is turning golden brown, then reduce the heat to moderate, 350°F/180°C/Gas Mark 4, and cook for a further 15–20 minutes. These are delicious eaten cold, but you can serve them warm if you like.

Apple and Pork Sausagemeat Puffed Roll

This is made in a fat roulade shape and I slice it thickly. It is vital to use the best pork sausages you can find – I recommend Marks & Spencer's free-range, or their butcher style, or their French style, all of which have a good high percentage of pork meat. (Quite why I haven't been invited to join the board of Marks & Spencer in all the years I've been praising their foodstuffs I can't work out;

perhaps the letter has got lost in the post!) The apples in the recipe aren't discernible as such, but they do complement the flavour of the sausagemeat so well, with the onions and thyme.

SERVES 6–8

---

2 tbsp sunflower oil
1½ lb/675 g pork sausages
* as described above, each*
* sausage slit down with a*
* sharp knife, and the skins*
* peeled off*
1 onion, skinned and finely
* chopped*
1 clove of garlic, skinned
* and finely chopped*
* (optional)*

3 good eating apples, e.g.
* Granny Smith's, peeled,*
* cored and diced*
A large pinch of dried
* thyme or the tiny leaves*
* stripped from a sprig of*
* fresh thyme*
A pinch of salt and freshly
* ground black pepper*
½ pt/285 ml dry cider
1½ lb/675 g puff pastry
Milk for glazing

Heat the oil in a sauté pan and cook the sausagemeat, mashing it with a wooden spoon to break it up from its sausage shape. When the sausagemeat is browned remove it, with a slotted spoon, to a warm dish. Add the onion and garlic, and the chopped apples to the sauté pan and cook till the onions are really soft – about 5 minutes. Replace the sausagemeat, and stir in the thyme, seasoning and cider. Let the mixture bubble gently till the liquid has reduced away. Then let the mixture cool.

To make the roll, roll out the puff pastry into two neat oblongs, each about 9 inches/23 cm long. Divide the sausage mixture between them, putting a line down the middle of each oblong, and leaving about an inch or so at either end. Brush the edges with milk, fold the short ends in, and pinch together the long ends in the centre of each roll. With two fish slices slip the rolls on to baking trays – no need to oil or butter the baking trays for puff pastry – and brush each roll with milk.

Bake in a hot oven, 425°F/220°C/Gas Mark 7, for 15–20 minutes, then lower the heat to 350°F/180°C/Gas Mark 4 and cook for a further 20–25 minutes, till well puffed up and deeply golden all over. Cool, then slice, before packing for the picnic. This is easiest transported on a tray or a rigid surface, wrapped in foil.

Ham Terrine with Quails' Eggs

This is a simple-to-make terrine, ideal to take for picnic eating, but I recommend slicing it first. Use good roast or boiled ham, not any processed ham. If you go to the small bother of flavouring the milk before you use it to make into the béchamel sauce it will really improve the overall flavour of the terrine. If you prefer, leave out the quails' eggs, but they are so much easier to find in shops these days, and they do add an interesting contrast in flavour and texture by their presence.

MAKES A TERRINE TO SERVE 6–8

1 pt/570 ml milk

1 onion, cut in half – skin and all)

1 stick of celery

A few peppercorns and a couple of bayleaves

2 oz/56 g butter

2 oz/56 g flour

1 tsp Dijon mustard

Freshly ground black pepper and grated nutmeg

¼ pt/140 ml vegetable, ham, or chicken stock

1 sachet of gelatine, or 4 leaves

1 lb/450 g roast or boiled ham, weighed when trimmed of fat, cut into bits, and whizzed briefly in a food processor till coarsely minced – you don't want it pulverized like baby food

¼ pt/140 ml double cream, whipped

Tabasco sauce

8 quails' eggs, boiled for 3 minutes, then cooled and shelled

Cut a strip of baking parchment to line the base and short ends of a 2 lb/900 g loaf tin.

Put the milk into a saucepan with the onion, celery, peppercorns and bayleaves, and put the pan on a moderate heat. Heat till a skin forms on the milk, then draw the pan off the heat and leave to cool. The ingredients will infuse the milk with their flavours. Strain the cooled milk.

Melt the butter in a clean saucepan and stir in the flour. Let it cook for a moment before adding the strained milk gradually, stirring till the sauce boils. Let it bubble for a minute, then take the pan off the heat. Season with the mustard, pepper and a grating of nutmeg. Warm the stock and sprinkle in the gelatine. Shake the pan gently till the granules of gelatine (or the leaves) dissolve completely, then stir this into the sauce. Wring out a piece of baking parchment in cold water and press it lightly on to the surface of the sauce – this prevents a skin forming as the sauce cools. When it is quite cold, but not set, mix in the coarsely minced ham. Fold in the whipped cream, taste, and add a dash of Tabasco at this stage if you like – I do!

Put half this mixture into the lined loaf tin and arrange the shelled quails' eggs in a line down the centre. Put the rest of the ham mixture on top. Bang the tin down a couple of times on a work surface, cover the tin with clingfilm, and leave overnight. Turn out by running a knife down either long side of the terrine. Turn it out on to a board or plate, peel off the strip of baking parchment, and slice the terrine thickly. Pack the slices, and transport in a thermal cold bag or box.

Pitta Bread with Grainy Mustard and Fillet of Beef

Pitta bread makes such a good alternative to bread as a container for sandwich filling. Pitta forms a natural 'pocket' for filling.

1 lb/450 g fillet of beef, cooked (I like to barbecue it for this) as rare as you like it, then the meat sliced in fine strips, then across, to produce fine dice	*1 crispheart lettuce, shredded finely* *½ pt/285 ml crème fraîche* *3–4 tsp mild grainy mustard – how much depends on your taste* *6 pitta breads*

Combine the ingredients and divide them between the six pitta 'pockets'. Wrap them in foil to transport. Fill them shortly before you leave, but you can make up the filling several hours in advance.

Pitta Bread with Chicken and Roast Red Pepper Mayonnaise

This is such a good filling – I think, for my taste, anyway! The garlic content is mild and sweet in flavour due to its roasting along with the red peppers. You can pulverize the peppers and garlic in with the mayonnaise, but I prefer to chop them. It really does matter to dice the chicken finely, and this is easy provided you have a really sharp knife. I love the Kitchen Devil knives.

2 red (or yellow, but not green) peppers *2–3 cloves of garlic, skinned and chopped* *2 tbsp olive oil* *3 chicken breasts, either roast or poached* *1 egg + 1 yolk* *½ tsp salt*	*½ tsp caster sugar* *A good grinding of black pepper* *½ tsp mustard powder* *¼ pt/140 ml oil – I mix extra virgin olive oil with sunflower oil* *3 tsp balsamic vinegar, or 2 tbsp wine vinegar* *6 pitta breads*

Start with the peppers. Cut each in half and scoop away the seeds. Put the peppers, skin side uppermost, under a red-hot grill, till their skins form great black blisters. Then put them into a polythene bag for 10 minutes, after which their skins should peel off easily. Chop them as neatly as you can, mix them with the chopped garlic and olive oil, and roast them in a hot oven for 10 minutes. Cool.

Slice each chicken breast into thin strips across, holding the breast with the flat of your hand, then slice it into thin strips down, then thinly slice it across again, which will give you finely diced chicken.

Put the egg, yolk, salt, sugar, pepper and mustard into a food processor and whiz, adding the oil drop by drop till it is all included. Lastly whiz in the vinegar.

Scrape the mayonnaise into a bowl. Fold in the cooled roast peppers and garlic, and the diced chicken. Divide the mixture evenly between the pitta breads.

Beef and Tomato Casserole

I usually think that tomatoes don't really complement beef very well – lamb, yes, but somehow beef needs something as well as tomatoes. In this casserole I hope I have found the answer in the red peppers, which add a sweetness to enhance the beef. It is a portable dish, and very good to eat on a winter picnic.

SERVES 6–8

2½ lb/1.1 kg stewing beef, weighed after having any excess fat and all gristle trimmed off
2 tbsp flour
Salt and plenty of freshly ground black pepper
3 red peppers

3–4 tbsp either sunflower or olive oil
2 onions, skinned and thinly sliced
1 clove of garlic, skinned and finely chopped
2 tins of chopped tomatoes (14 oz/400 g each)
1 pt/570 ml beef stock

Cut the trimmed beef into 1-inch/2.5-cm chunks, and put them into a polythene bag with the flour, salt and pepper. Shake all together well, so that each piece of beef is coated with seasoned flour.

Cut each pepper in half and scoop away the seeds. Put the pepper halves, skin side uppermost on a baking tray under a red-hot grill, till the skin forms great charred blisters. Then put the peppers into a polythene bag for 10 minutes, after which time the skins should peel off easily. Slice the skinned peppers.

Heat the oil in a heavy-based casserole and brown the floured meat, removing it with a slotted spoon, as it browns, to a warm dish. Then lower the heat a bit and add the sliced onions. Cook them, stirring occasionally, till they are really soft – about 5 minutes. Stir in the garlic, tomatoes and stock, and stir till it simmers. Then replace the browned meat, add the sliced peppers, cover with a lid, and cook in a moderate oven, 350°F/180°C/ Gas Mark 4 for 1½ hours.

Either keep it warm till you are ready to serve it, or cool it completely, store the casserole in a cold larder or the fridge, and reheat in a moderate oven till it is gently simmering. As with all stews and casseroles, this one improves its taste with reheating. Take baked jacket potatoes wrapped in two thicknesses of foil to eat with Beef and Tomato Casserole.

Jugged Hare with Forcemeat Balls

The best shooting lunch I ever ate was jugged hare with forcemeat balls. Whether it was the relief of coming into a barn and the comfort of sitting on the hay bales, and that anything would have tasted delicious on that day, I don't know, but I don't think so – I am sure it was the deliciousness of the jugged hare! I don't usually reckon anything gamey to be appropriate eating for a shoot lunch, but jugged hare is the exception. This transports as well as any other casserole or stew – in a dish in a thermal bag (and I think the best are to be found in Lakeland Plastics) with the forecemeat balls just wrapped in a double thickness of foil.

SERVES 6–8

1 large hare, cut into joints	*2 pared strips of lemon rind*
Seasoned flour	*+ 2 of orange rind (I use a*
2 oz/56 g butter + 2 tbsp	*potato peeler to do this, it*
sunflower oil	*avoids the risk of getting*
2 onions, each skinned and	*the bitter pith too)*
stuck with a few cloves	*2 oz/56 g plain flour*
3 carrots, peeled and	*2 pt/1.1 l water*
chopped	*3 tbsp redcurrant jelly*
2 sticks of celery, trimmed	*¼ pt/140 ml port*
and sliced	*As much blood from the*
1 clove of garlic, skinned	*hare as possible*
and chopped	

Coat each piece of hare in flour seasoned with salt and pepper. Heat the oil and melt the butter together in a heavy casserole and brown the pieces of hare on each side. Remove them to a warm dish. Add the onions to the oil and brown. Stir in the chopped carrots and sliced celery, the chopped garlic, lemon and orange rinds, and the flour. Cook for a minute or two, stirring to prevent anything from sticking. Then gradually add 2 pints/1.1 litres of water and the redcurrant jelly. Stir till the sauce simmers. Replace the joints of hare amongst the vegetables. Cover with a lid and cook in a moderate oven, 350°F/180°C/Gas Mark 4, for 1¾ hours.

Take the casserole out of the oven and cool enough to strip the meat from the bones. (You don't want to have to cope with bones at a lunch eaten out of doors.) Replace the hare meat in the casserole. Remove the onions and cloves. (You can do this a day in advance.) On top of the cooker, carefully (not too fast) reheat the casserole till it is gently simmering. Stir in the port. Ladle a small amount of hot hare gravy into the bowl with the hare blood and mix well. Stir this back into the casserole, taking great care not to let it simmer again once the blood has been added, in case it curdles.

To transport it, put a layer of foil on the bottom of a thermal bag to sit the dish or casserole containing the jugged hare.

Forcemeat Balls

These freeze beautifully, only needing to be reheated. I freeze them once I have fried them.

---

1 oz/28 g butter	*2 oz/56 g shredded suet*
1 onion, skinned and very finely chopped	*Grated rind of 1 lemon*
	Salt and pepper
4 oz/112 g day-old crumbs made from baked bread (as opposed to steamed sliced bread)	*Beaten egg and flour for coating*
	Sunflower oil for frying

Melt the butter in a small saucepan and sauté the chopped onion till it is really soft. Cool. Then mix it with the crumbs, suet, grated lemon rind and seasonings. Form into small balls, of even size, about the size of a ping-pong ball, and dip each in beaten egg, then in flour. Heat the oil in a non-stick frying pan and sauté the forcemeat balls, turning them so that they brown evenly. Once browned, put them on a dish with a double thickness of kitchen paper to absorb excess grease. Cool. Reheat in a low temperature oven for 20–25 minutes before wrapping them in foil to transport them.

Venison Pasty

This differs from the Game Pasty in that it is made with cold cooked venison – we always seem to have some left over from a roast haunch and it makes up into ideal picnic food as venison pasties.

Makes 8 pasties

3 tbsp sunflower oil + 2 oz/
56 g butter (I realize this
sounds rather a lot, but
the minced venison is
quite dry)

2 onions, skinned and finely
chopped

2 carrots, peeled and very
finely diced – easy with a
good sharp knife

1½ lb/675 g cold cooked and
trimmed venison, cut into
bits, then put into a food
processor and

whizzed till it is just
coarsely grated (or
minced) in appearance –
don't pulverize it too
finely

3 tsp tomato purée + 2 tbsp
Worcestershire sauce

½ pt/285 ml leftover gravy,
or 2 tsp flour + ½ pt/285
ml lager

Salt and pepper

1½ lb/675 g shortcrust
pastry

Heat the oil and melt the butter together in a heavy-based sauté pan. Add the chopped onions and diced carrots and cook over a moderate heat for several minutes, until when you stick a fork into a bit of carrot it feels tender. Stir in the minced venison, mix well, and stir in the tomato purée, Worcestershire sauce, flour (if you have no gravy) and, after a minute, the lager. Simmer all together gently for 10 minutes, then cool. Season with salt and pepper. Stir in the gravy, if you have some, after the tomato purée, instead of the flour.

Roll out the pastry and cut it into eight circles, each measuring about 6 inches/15cm in diameter. Put a good spoonful of the venison mixture down the middle of each circle. Brush the edges of the circle with milk and pinch them together. Very lightly butter a baking tray and put the pasties on this. Bake in a hot oven, 425°F/220°C/Gas Mark 7, for 15–20 minutes, or till the pastry turns golden, then reduce the heat to moderate, 350°F/180°C/Gas Mark 4, and cook for a further 15–20 minutes.

These are delicious cold, providing they are baked the same day that they are to be eaten. Alternatively, you can serve them warm.

Sausage Hot Pot

As with all food containing sausages, the quality of the sausages makes all the difference to the dish. (I do so hate metric and wish sausages were still packaged in 1-pound rather than 14-ounce packs!) This dish is halfway between a soup and a stew. It is very satisfying and makes ideal winter (or cold weather) picnic food.

SERVES 6–8

3–4 tbsp sunflower or olive oil

2 onions, skinned and thinly sliced

2 lb/900 g good pork sausages, cut into 1-inch/ 2.5-cm chunks; run the sharp blade of a knife down the sausages and remove their skins before cutting them

3 carrots, peeled and chopped into neat small dice

2 parsnips, peeled and cut as the carrots

3 leeks, washed well, trimmed and sliced thinly

Half a medium turnip, peeled and chopped into small dice

3 potatoes, peeled and cut into dice

1–2 cloves of garlic, skinned and chopped

8 oz/225 g red lentils

1½ pt/850 ml vegetable or chicken stock

Salt and pepper

Heat the oil in a heavy casserole and cook the sliced onions till they are soft and just beginning to turn golden. Then scoop them out and fry the chunks of sausage. If they break up as they brown it doesn't matter a bit. When the sausagemeat is fairly browned, replace the sautéed onions, stir in the rest of the prepared vegetables, the garlic, lentils and stock, and stir till the mixture just simmers. Add salt and pepper.

Cover with a lid and cook in a moderate oven, 350°F/180°C/Gas Mark 4, for 45–50 minutes, or till the bits of carrot are soft. You can reheat this without it spoiling in any way.

Irish Stew with Black Pudding

This dish appeared in my first book, *Seasonal Cooking*, but is such a wonderful dish that it must be included in this chapter. You really can't overcook it, but with this, almost more than with any other casserole, it is almost imperative that it be made, cooled and reheated. The flavour is so very much better.

SERVES 6–8

2 lb/900 g neck of lamb, with as much fat trimmed off as possible	3 onions, skinned and sliced
	6 carrots, peeled and sliced
½ lb/225 g black pudding, cut into dice about ⅓ inch/1 cm in size	6 fair-sized potatoes, peeled and sliced
	Salt and plenty of black pepper

Layer up the meat, black pudding and prepared vegetables in a heavy casserole, ending with a layer of potatoes. Season with salt and pepper. Pour in cold water to come level with the top of the last layer. Cover with a lid and cook in a moderate oven, 350°F/180°C/Gas Mark 4, for 2 hours, then reduce the temperature to 300°F/150°C/Gas Mark 2 and cook for a further hour. Take it out of the oven and cool completely. When it is cold, skim any fat off the surface. Cook for a further 1½ hours in a moderate oven, with the casserole without its lid for the last 45 minutes of cooking time.

Beef Stew with Root Vegetables and Mustard Dumplings

You don't need anything other than what is in this casserole. There is no need for jacket potatoes, or bread, because the combination of the meat, the variety of root vegetables and the mustard-flavoured dumplings with their hint of lemon, all go together so well, and in themselves provide the starch and protein and taste essential for a good and sustaining cold-weather picnic.

SERVES 6

---

4 tbsp sunflower or olive oil

2½ lb/1.1 kg stewing beef, trimmed of fat and gristle and cut into 1-inch/2.5-cm chunks

2 tbsp flour

Salt and black pepper

2 onions, skinned and chopped

1–2 cloves of garlic, skinned and chopped finely

2 carrots, peeled and chopped in chunky dice about ⅓ inch/1 cm in size

2 parsnips, peeled and cut as the carrots

Half a small turnip, peeled and cut as the carrots

2 leeks, washed, trimmed and sliced quite thinly

2 sticks of celery, washed, trimmed and sliced

2 beetroot, raw, peeled and chopped as the other root vegetables

2 pt/1.1 l stock, vegetable or beef (or use Baxter's consommé)

Heat the oil in a large and heavy casserole. Meanwhile shake the pieces of beef with the flour, salt and pepper in a large polythene bag till all the bits of beef are well coated. Brown the beef in the hot oil till it is all browned on all sides. Remove to a warm dish, using a slotted spoon to drip off as much oil as possible back into the casserole.

Cook the chopped onions in the oil, cooking till they are just beginning to turn golden. Stir in the garlic, cook for a minute, then add all the prepared vegetables. Pour in the stock, and stir till the stock simmers around the vegetables. Replace the browned meat amongst the vegetables, cover the casserole with its lid, and cook in a moderate oven, 350°F/180°C/Gas Mark 4, for 2 hours. Then take it out of the oven and cool it completely.

Reheat in a moderate oven till the contents simmer – about 30 minutes, providing you put the casserole in at room temperature, but add 20 minutes more if you put it in straight from the fridge. Let it cook from simmering point for a further 20 minutes before adding the dumplings, putting them on the surface of the stew and replacing the lid. Continue cooking the casserole for 45 minutes longer, with the dumplings.

Put a double layer of foil in the bottom of your thermal bag to transport the dish.

Mustard Dumplings

8 oz/225 g self-raising flour	*3 tsp dry mustard powder*
4 oz/112 g shredded suet	*½ tsp salt and a good*
Grated rind of 1 lemon	*grinding of black pepper*
	Cold water

Mix all the dry ingredients together well, then add just enough cold water to bind to a stiff dough. Flour your hands (to stop the dough sticking to them) and shape the dough into even-sized blobs. Push them down amongst the hot contents in the casserole, replace the lid, and replace the casserole in the moderate oven for a further 45 minutes.

Cottage Pie with Julienne Vegetables on top

People often confuse a cottage pie with a shepherd's pie. As I have always understood it, the two are quite different – the cottage pie is made with raw minced beef (or venison) and the shepherd's with leftover cooked lamb. This pie is made with minced raw beef. As I don't like to buy ready minced beef, I buy lean stewing steak (rump steak, in Scotland) and whiz it in my food processor. If you do this too, you have to watch out not to over-pulverize the beef, just whiz it till it is coarsely ground.

The thin strips of root vegetables on top of this pie negate the need for any accompaniment – everything is in the one dish. As you may not have a sufficiently large thermally insulated bag to keep it hot, line a suitably sized cardboard box with several layers of foil and transport the dish in that, also covered with foil.

If you have a mandolin, that will take the effort out of cutting the julienne strips.

SERVES 6–8

3–4 tbsp olive oil
3 carrots peeled and sliced into as fine julienne strips as you can cut, about 2 inches/5 cm long
2 parsnips, cut as the carrots
Half a turnip, peeled and cut as the carrots
2 heads of celeriac, peeled and cut as the carrots
Salt and pepper
4 tbsp olive oil

2½ lb/1.1 kg lean beef, trimmed of fat and whizzed to a coarse ground state
2 onions, skinned and finely chopped
2 tbsp flour
2 tbsp tomato purée
1½ pt/850 ml water and lager mixed
Salt and pepper
2 tbsp day-old breadcrumbs mixed with 3 oz/84 g grated Cheddar cheese

In a large sauté pan heat 3–4 tbsp of oil and cook the prepared vegetables for the top over a moderate heat, stirring from time to time, for about 10 minutes – a piece of carrot, when stuck with a fork, should feel barely tender. Season with salt and pepper. Set on one side.

In another sauté pan, or in a saucepan with a wide base, heat the other 4 tbsp of oil and cook the minced or ground beef till it is brown. With a slotted spoon remove it to a warm dish. Cook the chopped onions in the saucepan till they are really soft – about 5 minutes. Then stir in the flour and cook for a minute longer before stirring in the tomato purée, water and lager, and salt and pepper. Stir till this mixture simmers gently. Put the browned meat back in amongst the onions and tomatoey sauce, cover the pan with a lid and let it simmer very gently for 20 minutes, stirring it from time to time to prevent it sticking. Then pour it into a fairly deep pie dish. Spoon the sautéed root vegetables over the surface.

Scatter the grated cheese and breadcrumbs over the vegetables, and bake in a moderate oven, 350°F/180°C/Gas Mark 4 for 35–40 minutes. The top should be fairly crisply browned.

Venison (or Pork) Sausages with Braised Red Cabbage and Baked Jacket Potatoes

This is a very portable picnic menu for a chilly day out. Choose the type of sausage you like – for my taste it is pork, with the highest percentage of pork meat that I can buy. But you can buy delicious venison sausages made by MacBeth's, the butcher's shop in Forres, who also do mail order. I grill the sausages to the degree of brownness which I like, which is very well grilled, then I wrap them in foil. I wrap the baked jacket potatoes in foil, separately, and I transport the braised red cabbage with its apples and onions and its hint of juniper in a dish in an insulated thermal bag. Don't forget to take butter separately, for eating with the potatoes. I find it easier to cut the butter into generous bits before I put it in with the picnic things.

Braised Red Cabbage

SERVES 6–8

3 tbsp sunflower or olive oil	*chopped*
2 onions, skinned and chopped finely	*About 5–6 juniper berries, crushed*
1 average-sized red cabbage, chopped neatly	*Salt and pepper*
	1 tsp soft brown sugar
4 good eating apples, e.g Cox's, peeled cored and	*2 tbsp white wine vinegar, or 2 tsp Balsamic vinegar*

Heat the oil and cook the chopped onions till they are soft and just beginning to turn golden at the edges. Add the cabbage and apples and the juniper berries.

Cook, stirring occasionally, for about 5 minutes. Then stir in the seasonings and the vinegar.

Cover with a lid, and cook on a gentle heat for 25–30 minutes, taking the lid off from time to time to give it all a good stir, to prevent sticking. This reheats successfully, if you have any left over.

Thick Venison and Vegetable Soup

This soup is a meal in itself. It is simplicity itself to make; the time spent is in the vegetable preparation. I think it benefits from being made, cooled, and reheated. As with all casseroles or stews, the flavours in this soup improve.

SERVES 6–8

4 tbsp sunflower or olive oil	*Half a turnip, peeled and*
2 lb/900 g venison, trimmed	*cut small neat cubes*
of all gristle and the meat	*4 potatoes, peeled and diced*
sliced into small dice;	*2 leeks, washed, trimmed*
alternatively, you could	*and sliced finely*
briefly whiz it in a food	*Salt and pepper*
processor	*1 tsp sugar*
2 onions, each skinned and	*About ½ tsp dried thyme,*
chopped finely	*or the tiny leaves stripped*
1–2 cloves of garlic, skinned	*off a sprig*
and chopped finely	*3 pt/1.7 l good beef, game,*
4 sticks of celery, trimmed	*or vegetable stock*
and sliced thinly	

Heat the oil in a large saucepan and brown the meat all over on a high heat. Add the onions and cook for a further 5 minutes. Then stir in all the other ingredients, add the stock, bring to simmering point, cover tightly with a lid, and cook in the oven at 200°F/ 120°C/Gas Mark ½ for 2½–3 hours. If you have an Aga, it won't hurt if you leave it in the top left oven overnight.

Children's Lunches

Baked Jacket Potatoes with (a) Coleslaw Filling
(b) Tuna and Cheese Filling

Pasta with Cheese and Crispy Bacon

Fishcakes

Toad in the Hole with Onion Gravy

Ham, Parsley and Cheese Tart

Shepherd's Pie

Smoked Haddock and Leek Pasta

Meatballs in Tomato Sauce

Chicken Breasts Baked with Mushrooms

Fish Stir-Fried with Leeks and Ginger

Smoked Haddock and Bread Soufflé

Sausages in Pinhead Oatmeal

Marinated Sausages

Homemade Hamburgers

CHILDREN'S LUNCHES

The fact that this is a chapter with suggestions for lunches for children doesn't mean that no other recipe in the book is suitable for children. Far from it. With four children of our own, it is my experience that most children love all types of food. Some, on the other hand, really do not like certain foods. For example, two of ours love all offal, whereas the other two (I find it hard to remember which – maddening, when planning what to eat, to have such an abysmal memory!) really dislike offal in its various guises. I can't bear, though, children who say they 'can't' eat something when they haven't even tried it – my tolerance is very low! But there are certain foods universally loved by nearly all children, and hopefully these are here in this chapter.

You must forgive my including some items, such as Hamburgers and Fishcakes, which I know are in my book *Suppers*, but it seems dotty to have a chapter on children's lunches and not to include such children's staples. As far as children are concerned you are always on safe ground with chicken. But there are a number of children who love fish, and pasta, too, is very popular. Meriel, our third daughter, makes Toad in the Hole whenever we have it, because of my complete inability to make an edible Yorkshire pudding, to my enduring shame. (See the chapter on Sunday lunches.) Meriel makes a very fine Toad! Fishcakes are tremendously popular, and convenient, because you can make a batch and freeze them. The Sausages in Pinhead Oatmeal are delicious – filling, and I don't usually bother to have potatoes with them. A certain amount of the oatmeal falls off them during their cooking, but this doesn't matter – enough stays on to give a good crunch.

There are two suggested fillings for the baked potato – I love both and both seem to be universally loved. So I hope that there will be something in this chapter which will help you, should you be stuck for an idea for lunch when feeding one or more children!

Baked Jacket Potatoes

As with so many recipes, how many potatoes you allow per person depends entirely on the age of the child. One large potato is enough for all girls and most boys till they become ravenous teenagers, when it is safer to allow two per person.

Split the baked potatoes lengthways before spooning in the filling.

Coleslaw Filling

What I can't bear in a true coleslaw is the raw onion. However, a small amount of raw red onion is delicious, being much milder in flavour. If you prefer to use a mayonnaise binding sauce do, but I like this creamy fromage frais base to my coleslaw.

SERVES 6

Half a white cabbage, shredded as finely as you can and then chopped – small children in particular don't like eating long shreds	*Half a red onion, skinned and very finely chopped* *1 apple, peeled, cored and grated* *1 tub (7 fl oz/200 ml) of creamy fromage frais*

Mix together all the above ingredients and leave them in a covered container for at least 2 hours before serving. This allows the flavours to blend together.

Tuna and Cheese Filling

SERVES 6

2 cans of tuna, 6½ oz/185g each, drained of oil and the fish mashed in a bowl	*4 tbsp good mayonnaise* *3 oz/84 g, grated Cheddar cheese* *2 tsp lemon juice*

Mix together the above ingredients. If you like, stir in 1–2 table-spoons of finely chopped parsley, which gives some vitamin C content to the filling.

Pasta with Cheese and Crispy Bacon

This is a more interesting version of that old stand-by, macaroni cheese. A cheese sauce can be made very much more definite in its flavour by adding mustard to the roux, and balsamic vinegar to the sauce, neither of which will in any way be identifiable. The crispy bacon crumbled into the sauce at the last minute makes a good contrast in flavour and a crunch in texture.

SERVES 6

2 oz/56 g butter	*A grating of nutmeg*
1 onion, skinned and finely chopped	*12 oz/340 g pasta – I often use pasta shells when making*
2 oz/56 g flour less 2 tsp	*this (more if you are feeding*
2 tsp mustard powder	*teenagers with large*
1¼ pt/710 ml milk	*appetites, say 18 oz/510 g)*
4 oz/112 g good Cheddar cheese, grated	*1 tbsp olive oil*
2 tsp balsamic vinegar	*6 rashers of streaky bacon, grilled till crisp, then*
Salt and freshly ground black pepper	*broken into bits as small as you can*

Melt the butter and sauté the chopped onion in it till it is very soft and just beginning to turn golden. Stir in the flour and mustard. Let this cook for a minute, then gradually add the milk, stirring all the time till the sauce boils. Draw the pan off the heat and stir in the cheese, balsamic vinegar, salt, pepper and nutmeg to your taste. Stir till the cheese melts. Cover closely with a dampened piece of baking parchment, to prevent a skin forming.

Meanwhile, cook the pasta in plenty of boiling salted water, till when you stick your – clean – thumbnail into a piece of pasta it feels tender. This is the stage known as *al dente* – overcooked pasta is slimy. Drain the pasta, then toss it in a tablespoon of olive oil, which will help prevent it from sticking together.

Serve as immediately as you can, stirring the crispy bacon through the sauce just before spooning it over each helping of pasta. Alternatively, you can stir the pasta and sauce on to the plates. The hot pasta will reheat the sauce when it is stirred into it.

Fishcakes

This recipe could well fit in any of the chapters (possibly not the Puddings chapter . . .) but I find that fishcakes are a hit with all age groups. I think there are two reasons for this: one is that most people find anything with a crispy texture appealing, and the other is that I make fishcakes (and fish pie, too, for that matter) with smoked fish. Unsmoked fish, for my taste, just hasn't sufficient flavour for fishcakes. The worst type of fish is salmon. Far too many people think that salmon fishcakes are a ritzier version of the humbler but far more delicious fishcake made with smoked haddock. Twice-cooked salmon is dry and pretty well tasteless.

Fishcakes belong in this chapter because they have particular child appeal. They are also very convenient in that they can be made ahead, and even made in advance and frozen. They only take a couple of hours at room temperature to thaw before being shallow fried. There is no need to toast the breadcrumbs before you coat the fishcakes, because the fresh crumbs crisp up anyway as the fishcakes fry. But I much prefer to use my own homemade crumbs rather than those bought ones, which used to come in a hideous shade of bright orange but are now more subdued in hue.

2 lb/900 g smoked haddock
Milk to cover the fish in the
*   saucepan*
2 lb/900 g potatoes, weighed
*   when peeled, boiled till*
*   tender, then mashed well*
2–3 tbsp finely chopped
*   parsley – this is*
*   important, it really*
*   improves the appearance*

of the fishcakes once they
*   are cut open*
Freshly ground black pepper
Flour for dusting
2 eggs, beaten, on a plate
About 6 oz/170 g day-old
*   baked bread, whizzed to*
*   fine crumbs*
Sunflower oil + butter for
*   frying*

Feel the raw fish all over on a board. Remove any bones you feel – this is the only sure way to find bones and to be able to reassure those eating the fishcakes that they are truly bone-free. Cut the fish into bits and put them into a saucepan. Cover with milk, and over moderate heat bring to a gentle simmer. Take the pan off the heat and leave the fish to cool in the milk.

Strain the milk, when cold (use it to make smoked haddock flavoured soup, using sautéed onions and diced potatoes as the bulk of the soup), and mash the cooked fish into the potatoes, adding a small amount of milk – you have to be careful not to make the potato and fish mixture too damp to form into fishcakes. Beat in the parsley and the pepper. Dip your hand in flour and form the mixture into cake shapes of even size. Dip each into beaten egg, then into the crumbs, coating each cake on each side. Put them on to a tray lined with baking parchment. Cover the finished trayful with clingfilm and either store in the fridge till you are ready to fry them, or freeze them.

To fry them, heat a small amount of sunflower oil and melt butter – in a non-stick frying pan, if at all possible, because that way you use much less oil. Fry them till they are golden brown on each side. As they cook, remove them from the frying pan to a dish lined with kitchen paper to absorb excess grease. They are very good with tomato sauce, homemade, or ketchup. There is no need for added potato, rice, or pasta, but a salad or green vegetable is good.

Toad in the Hole with Onion Gravy

I mentioned in the introduction to this chapter the fact that Meriel makes Toad in the Hole for our family – she is our third daughter, aged 17 at the time of writing. We all love anything to do with Yorkshire pudding, but I wish I could make a Yorkshire pud which is edible. My contribution to supper or lunch, when Toad in the Hole is the main part, is the Onion Gravy, which, as far as our family are concerned, is an integral part of the meal. For health, a green vegetable is essential. Stir-fried cabbage with grainy mustard is the perfect accompaniment for this dish.

SERVES 6

1½ lb/675 g good pork
   sausages, each cut in half,
   or chipolatas
6 oz/170 g plain flour sieved
   with a pinch of salt and

freshly ground pepper
3 large eggs
½ pt/285 ml milk with
   2 tbsp cold water

Grill the sausages or chipolatas till browned – I can't bear the anaemic appearance of ungrilled sausages in Toad or any other dish containing sausages. Put them into a Pyrex or similarly ovenproof dish along with about 2 tablespoons of the fat which has come from them as they grill.

Put all the other ingredients into a food processor or liquidizer and whiz. Leave the batter to sit for 30 minutes before pouring it into the sausages. Cook in a very hot oven – 425°F/220°C/Gas Mark 7, for about 30–35 minutes, or till the Hole is well puffed up and golden brown. If you cook it in a metal container it will cook quicker – you will need about 5 minutes less cooking time.

Onion Gravy

Ideally, some beef dripping,
about 2 tbsp; as a
dripping substitute,
2 tbsp sunflower oil + 1
oz/28 g butter
2 onions, skinned and very
finely sliced
2 cloves of garlic, skinned
and chopped finely –

optional, but we love
garlic and tend to put it
in everything
1 rounded tbsp flour
1 pt/570 ml chicken, beef, or
vegetable stock
Gravy browning if you think
a deeper colour is more
attractive
Salt and pepper to taste

Melt the dripping or heat the oil and melt the butter together in a saucepan and sauté the sliced onions very well, stirring from time to time, till they are really soft and turning dark golden brown. This takes about 7–10 minutes to do properly, but try not to hurry the procedure because it makes all the difference to the taste of the gravy. Then stir in the garlic and the flour. Let it cook for a moment before stirring in the stock, stirring till the gravy boils. Draw the saucepan off the heat, add the gravy browning if you like, and season with salt and pepper to your taste.

Ham, Parsley and Cheese Tart

I made this for lunch one day years ago when we had a gang of children for the day – it must have been a Saturday – and it was greeted with acclaim. It has been requested by one or other of our children ever since. It is so easy, but like all savoury tarts the filling is much nicer made with a higher quantity of egg yolk to whole eggs – it gives the custard a much softer texture.

SERVES 6

For the pastry:

4 oz/112 g butter, hard from the fridge, cut into bits

6 oz/170 g plain flour + 1 tsp icing sugar

½ tsp each of salt and black pepper

For the filling:

1 lb/450 g boiled or baked ham, trimmed of fat and gristle and cut into slivers

2 large eggs + the yolks of 2 large eggs

½ pt/285 ml milk – as creamy as possible

Pepper – the ham will be salty enough for most tastes

2 tbsp chopped parsley and snipped chives, mixed

3 oz/84 g grated Cheddar cheese

Put all the ingredients for the pastry into a processor and whiz till the mixture resembles fine crumbs. Pat this firmly around the sides and base of a 9 inch/23 cm flan dish. Put the dish into the fridge for an hour minimum, then bake in a moderate oven, 350°F/180°C/Gas Mark 4, for 20–25 minutes, till the pastry is golden brown at the edges.

Make the filling by scattering the sliced ham over the base of the cooked pastry, and beating together the eggs and yolks with the milk. Season with pepper, stir in the chopped parsley and snipped chives, and pour into the pastry case, over the ham. Scatter the grated cheese over the top – most will sink down into the liquid, but it doesn't matter. Bake in the moderate oven, as for the pastry, for 15–20 minutes, or till when you gently shake the flan dish the filling barely wobbles in the centre – the centre is the last part to 'set'. Take it out of the oven and serve warm. It also makes good eating served cold, and it is then very portable picnic food. All you need to accompany it is a salad.

Shepherd's Pie

A properly made Shepherd's Pie is one of the best dishes I know, for child or adult. But I read recipes for Shepherd's Pie using raw meat, which is *not* what I have always understood to be proper. Real Shepherd's Pie should always be make with leftover roast lamb, although I sometimes use roast venison or roast beef. As I understand it, a similar pie made with raw minced beef is known as a Cottage Pie, and, for my taste, has a much less appealing taste, when the exception, of course, of the recipe in my Packed and Picnic Lunches section. Good Shepherd's Pie should be really well flavoured with the ingredients you see in the recipe – tomato purée, well sautéed onions, Worcestershire sauce, and I like to add a teaspoon of redcurrant jelly. It is such an ideal dish for every age group, but particularly so when feeding a group of children of different ages, because almost toothless young children can eat the minced meat base and well-beaten mashed potato top of a good Shepherd. And don't worry about the flavourings – it is a real failing of we British that we tend to omit such items from our cooking for children in the fear that the taste will be too strong for them. I reckon that the earlier children are brought up to eat every flavour I can think of, the better adjusted their palates will be. Think of the French and the Italians, whose children are weaned on to adult foods.

SERVES 6

About 2 lb/900 g potatoes
1/2 pt/285 ml warm milk
2 oz/56 g butter
Salt and pepper
2 tbsp of lamb dripping, or
    4 tbsp olive oil
1 onion, skinned and
    chopped finely
1 1/2 lb/675 g leftover roast
    lamb (or beef, or venison)
    weighed after having been
    trimmed of all fat

and gristle; put the cut-up
    meat into a processor and
    whiz, but not too finely
1 fairly level tbsp flour
1 tbsp tomato purée
1 tsp redcurrant jelly
3 tbsp Worcestershire sauce
    (or 3 tsp balsamic
    vinegar)
1 pt/570 ml lamb, beef, or
    vegetable stock
Butter for finishing

Peel the potatoes and boil them in salted water till you can easily stick a fork into the biggest bit. Drain them well, shaking the pan over heat to steam any excess water off the drained potatoes. Mash them well, then, with a wooden spoon, beat them well, adding the warm milk and butter. Season to taste with salt and pepper.

Make the Shepherd part of the pie by melting the dripping in a heavy based saucepan or casserole, or heating the oil. Cook the chopped onion over gentle heat till it is turning golden brown at the edges. Then raise the heat and stir in the processed lamb (or beef, or venison), adding the flour, tomato purée and redcurrant jelly. Cook for 2 or 3 minutes, taking care not to let the mixture stick to the bottom of the pan. Then stir in the Worcestershire sauce and the stock, and keep stirring till the contents of the pan reach simmering point. Taste, and add salt and pepper. Let this mixture simmer very gently for 10 minutes, then put it into a pie dish and let it cool.

When the base is cold, put the well-beaten potato over the top, using a fork to make long furrowed lines all over the surface. Put little dots of butter over the top of the potato, or alternatively you can brush melted butter over the entire surface of the potato. Reheat in a moderate oven, 350°F/180°C/Gas Mark 4, for 40–45 minutes, or till the meat mixture is bubbling at the edges and the top of the potato is golden brown.

I like a vegetable in creamy white sauce, such as cauliflower or leeks, to go with this Shepherd's Pie.

Smoked Haddock and Leek Pasta

Leeks and smoked fish go together awfully well. Bound together in a sauce made with milk in which the fish cooked, this makes a really good sauce for pasta. Use any small shaped (as opposed to long pasta, like spaghetti or fettucine) pasta, such as shells or bows, for this dish.

1 lb/450 g smoked haddock,	*Freshly ground black pepper*
the undyed fish	*and, if you like, a grating*
1 pt/570 ml milk	*of nutmeg – the fish will*
2 oz/56 g butter	*have enough saltiness for*
4 leeks, washed well,	*most people's tastes*
trimmed and sliced thinly	*12 oz/340 g pasta (or more,*
2 oz/56 g flour	*depending on appetites)*

Feel the fish all over and remove any bones you feel. Cut it into smallish pieces and put it into a saucepan with the milk. Over a moderate heat heat the milk till a skin forms, then take the pan off the heat and let the fish cool in the milk.

Meanwhile, in another saucepan melt the butter. Add the sliced leeks and cook till they are really soft. Then stir in the flour, let it cook for a minute, then gradually add the strained fish milk, stirring till the sauce boils. Draw the pan off the heat, season with pepper and nutmeg, and stir in the fish. Cover closely with dampened baking parchment, to prevent a skin forming.

Cook the pasta in plenty of boiling salted water till a piece of pasta feels just tender when you stick your – clean – thumbnail into it. Drain well and mix in the sauce. Serve as soon as you can, to avoid the pasta cooking further in the hot sauce.

Meatballs in Tomato Sauce

When you make your own meatballs you can turn a mundane dish into something really special. I like to use half beef – and as for hamburgers, I buy rump steak and pulverize it in the food processor rather than buy ready minced beef – and half good quality pork sausagemeat. The sausagemeat keeps the meatballs juicy and the flavours of both meats and the other ingredients make a delicious combination. The meatballs freeze very well in their tomatoey sauce. The only drawback is that you always need more meatballs than you imagine you will. They really are a hit with nearly all children.

SERVES 6

1½ lb/675 g rump steak, trimmed of excess fat and all gristle

2 tbsp olive oil

2 onions, skinned and as finely chopped as you can manage

1½ lb/675 g best quality pork sausages, each slit with a sharp knife and the skins peeled off – this takes seconds

2 tbsp finely chopped parsley and snipped chives, mixed

A dash of Tabasco sauce

A couple of pinches of salt and freshly ground black pepper

Flour for dusting

Olive oil for frying the meatballs – you need little oil if you have a non-stick pan

---

Put the trimmed beef into a processor and pulverize, but not too finely. Heat the olive oil in a saucepan and gently fry the finely chopped onions till they are really soft – this takes about 5 minutes. Let them cool completely. With your hand, mix together the skinned sausagemeat and the pulverized beef, and mix in the cooled onions, parsley and chives, Tabasco, salt and pepper.

Have a bowl of flour to dip your hands into as you form the mixture into small balls, about the size of a ping-pong ball. Roll each in flour and lay them on a baking parchment lined tray. When you have made up the mixture into meatballs, heat the olive oil in a frying or sauté pan, using as little oil as you can, and fry the meatballs, turning them carefully (I use two forks for the turning) so that they brown all over. As they brown, remove them to a large warm plate lined with a couple of thicknesses of kitchen paper, to absorb excess grease. When all are made cover them with Tomato Sauce.

Tomato Sauce

3 tbsp olive oil	1–2 cloves of garlic, skinned
2 onions, skinned and	and finely chopped
chopped	3 cans (15 oz/420 g) of
1 stick of celery, trimmed	chopped tomatoes
and sliced	Salt, pepper and a pinch of
	sugar

Heat the oil and gently sauté the chopped onions and sliced celery in the oil till the onion is soft and just beginning to turn golden brown. Then add the chopped garlic (for a more pronounced garlic taste – if you prefer a milder taste add the garlic at the beginning of the onions' cooking time) and sauté for a few seconds. Stir in the contents of the cans of tomatoes, and season with salt, pepper and sugar. With the lid off the pan, simmer this sauce gently for 20 minutes. Then cool and liquidize the sauce – check the seasoning and add more salt and pepper if you think it needs it.

Pour the sauce over the meatballs, in an ovenproof dish, and reheat, with the dish covered, in a moderate oven, 350°F/180°C/ Gas Mark 4, for 30–35 minutes. This will take longer if the dish has come straight out of the fridge, or if the dish is covered with foil as its lid. Reheat till the sauce is gently bubbling around the meatballs.

Freeze the meatballs before the cooking, if you make them up and cover them with the sauce in advance. Allow them to thaw overnight in the fridge.

Chicken Breasts Baked with Mushrooms

Chicken, in whatever form, is universally popular with children. Whenever one of ours is given the choice of what to make for lunch or supper, the decision is invariably chicken in some form or other. This baked chicken dish is simplicity itself to make, and how much garlic you include depends entirely on the general fondness for garlic in your family – with all of us, our liking for garlic amounts almost to addiction.

The ideal accompaniments for this baked chicken dish are either baked jacket potatoes, or steamed (or boiled) new potatoes, with a green salad.

SERVES 6

---

3 tbsp olive oil	*¹/₂ lb/225 g mushrooms,*
6 chicken breasts, with the	*wiped, stalks trimmed,*
skin on (it helps prevent	*and sliced*
shrinkage in cooking)	*Scant tbsp flour*
2 onions, skinned and finely	*1 pt/570 ml chicken stock*
sliced, or chopped if you	*Salt and freshly ground*
prefer	*black pepper*
1–2 cloves of garlic, skinned	*¹/₄ pt/140 ml double cream*
and finely chopped	

Heat the oil in a heavy sauté pan and brown the chicken breasts on their skin sides. Remove them, once browned, to a warm dish. Gently sauté the sliced onions till they are really soft – this takes about 5 minutes. Then add the chopped garlic and the sliced mushrooms to the pan – you may need to add more olive oil as the mushrooms tend to take up a lot of oil – sauté for a couple of minutes before stirring in the flour. After a further minute's cooking time stir in the stock and keep stirring till the sauce simmers. Replace the browned chicken breasts in the gently simmering sauce, skin side uppermost. Cover with a lid and bake for 30 minutes in a moderate oven, 350°F/180°C/Gas Mark 4.

Take the sauté pan out of the oven and put it back on a gentle heat. Season with salt and pepper to your taste, and stir in the cream – there is no fear of curdling with double cream, so don't worry. Serve as soon as you like, but this dish will keep warm very satisfactorily in a low temperature oven for 20–30 minutes.

Fish Stir-Fried with Leeks and Ginger

Improbable as this dish may sound in a chapter of recipes I deem suitable for children's lunches, I am putting it in because we have this often and it is an extremely popular dish not only with our own children but with any of their friends who like fish. Don't be put off by the leeks and ginger – the heat of the ginger is so decreased in its cooking and its flavour goes so very well with that of the leeks, that they both complement the fish very well, if surprisingly so.

I like to serve this with plain boiled Basmati rice, into which I stir lots of chopped parsley to make it look more interesting.

SERVES 6

2 lb/900 g firm-fleshed white fish, such as hake; cod will do, but it will fall into flakes as it cooks	*4 leeks, washed well, trimmed and sliced thinly*
1 tsp cornflour	*About 1 inch/2.5 cm fresh ginger, its skin pared off and the ginger chopped or grated as finely as you can*
3 tbsp dark soy sauce	
2 tsp sesame oil	
1 pt/570 ml vegetable stock	*1 clove of garlic, skinned and chopped finely*
3 tbsp sunflower oil	

First, put the fish on a board and feel it all over to find bones. Remove them. Then cut the fish into 1-inch/2.5-cm bits.

Mix the cornflour with the soy sauce, sesame oil and stock. Then, in a large heavy-based sauté pan heat the sunflower oil and stir fry the leeks, chopped ginger and chopped garlic till the leeks are really soft – about 5 minutes over a moderately high heat. When you are sure the sliced leeks are really soft, add the cut-up fish and stir in the cornflour liquid. Cook over high heat till the sauce bubbles. The fish will then be cooked, too. Serve as soon as possible, to prevent the fish overcooking in the heat of the sauce.

Smoked Haddock and Bread Soufflé

This isn't a soufflé in the strictly accurate sense, but it is a most useful and delicious dish which does puff up as it cooks. It is also very convenient in that it has to be made the day before it is to be cooked – the bread soaks up the milk and eggs mixture and isn't discernible as bread in the baked dish. It is also useful in that you only need accompany it with a salad, either green or tomato.

SERVES 6

6 slices good baked brown bread, crusts removed, each slice buttered and cut into about 1-inch/2.5-cm cubes	*1½ lb/675 g smoked haddock* *1½ pt/850 ml milk* *4 large eggs + 2 yolks* *Freshly ground black pepper*

Butter an ovenproof dish, Pyrex or similar, capable of holding 3–4 pints/1.7–2.3 litres. Put the buttered cubes of brown bread in the bottom of the dish.

Put the fillets of smoked haddock on a board and feel each one, removing any bones you feel. This is the only sure way of removing all fish bones. Cut the fish into 1-inch/2.5-cm chunks and put them into a saucepan with the milk. Heat to the point where the milk forms a skin, then take the pan off the heat and leave the fish to cool in the milk. When cooled, scoop out the pieces of fish with a slotted spoon and put them over the bread in the dish. Beat together the eggs and yolks, and the fish milk. Season with pepper – no need for salt, the fish will add enough saltiness – and pour this liquid over the fish and bread. Cover the dish with clingfilm and store it in the fridge overnight.

Bake in a moderate oven, 350°F/180°C/Gas Mark 4, for 40–45 minutes, or till the contents of the dish are puffed up, golden and firm when you shake the dish. Eat as soon as you can.

Sausages in Pinhead Oatmeal

Our son, Hugo (aged 14 at the time of writing), came home from school for half term and said that we should try cooking sausages like his friend Fergus Maclay has them at home. To use Hugo's description, the sausages are 'peeled' and rolled in oatmeal. So we had a go and made them for supper one night. As with all dishes using sausages, for me it is vital to use as good sausages as you can buy. Those with the highest percentage of meat, rather than pork, are the best. There is an excellent Italian delicatessen in Edinburgh called Valvona & Crolla which sells 100 per cent pork meat sausages, and they are the best!

If you have any trouble finding pinhead oatmeal look for it in a health food shop. It makes a delicious coating for chicken pieces and filleted fish as well as for these sausages.

FOR 2 LB/900 G SAUSAGES

---

1 beaten egg
6–8 oz/170–225 g pinhead oatmeal
Sunflower oil for frying

With a sharp knife slit each sausage lengthwise and peel off the skins. This doesn't take a second. Roll each skinned sausage in beaten egg, then in the oatmeal. Put them on to a tray lined with baking parchment till you are ready to cook them. Fry them in a small amount of sunflower oil, turning them (I find two forks easiest for this) so that they end up golden brown all over.

A certain amount of the pinhead oatmeal will fall off during the cooking, but enough will stick to give a good crunchy coating to the sausages. They are delicious, but filling, and I think potatoes are superfluous, but Hugo doesn't agree! So mashed potatoes for those who like, and a green vegetable like steamed cabbage is good with these sausages – or baked beans, but I find the combination altogether too filling.

Marinated Sausages

Whenever I am cooking sausages I buy those with the highest percentage of meat, as opposed to pork, content I can find. These sausages can just be baked, or they can be barbecued. Don't be put off by the ginger in the simple marinade – believe me, children do love them.

Stab each sausage in as many places as you can, to allow the marinade to seep into the casings and into the meat. For youngish children I allow two sausages per person. Any left over are delicious eaten cold.

For 1 lb/450 g sausages

For the marinade:

2 tbsp sesame oil

4 tbsp sunflower oil

4 tsp sesame seeds, toasted by shaking them in a dry pan over heat till they turn biscuit coloured

½ inch/2.5 cm fresh ginger, skin pared off and the ginger very finely chopped

2 tbsp dark soy sauce

Shake together the ingredients for the marinade and pour this over the sausages in a dish. Marinate for 24 hours if possible, turning the sausages over in the marinade when you remember. Bake them, or grill them, or barbecue them.

They are good with crispy sautéed potatoes. Parboil small potatoes, new or old, with their skins on, then drain them well and chop them into chunks about 1 inch/2.5 cm in size. Sauté in olive oil and salt over a moderate heat in a heavy-based pan (ideally a Wol pan) till golden brown all over. Keep them warm on a dish lined with several thicknesses of kitchen paper, to absorb excess oil. Serve peeled carrots cut into sticks, for health!

Homemade Hamburgers

To repeat the point I made in my last book, *Suppers*, I have a horror of bought hamburgers because of the uncertainty of their content. That is why I much prefer to make my own, buying the beef from our excellent butcher here in Skye, and whizzing the meat in the processor to the degree of groundness that I like, which is not too fine. Over-pulverized, the meat becomes bouncy in texture when grilled or chargrilled. With a coarse texture the cooked hamburger has a much more pleasing texture to eat. I find that if I have a bowl of cold water to hand whilst I make the meat into hamburger shapes, repeated plunging of my hands into the water makes this a much less messy task – the meat doesn't stick to dampened hands nearly as much as it does to dry ones.

I like these best served in buttered buns, with Heinz tomato ketchup (only Heinz will do, all others have artificial ingredients added to them), bowls of salad and bowls of crisps.

Allow one hamburger each for small children, but older ones will eat two; make the hamburgers a bit smaller for two per person consumption.

SERVES 6

2 lb/900 g lean steak – I use rump	Salt and freshly ground black pepper
1 egg, beaten	1 onion, skinned and very finely chopped
2 tsp balsamic vinegar	2 tbsp olive oil

Trim excess fat and any gristle off the meat and cut it into chunks. Put it into the processor and whiz till it is ground, but coarsely. Briefly, so as not to over-pulverize the meat, whiz in the egg, balsamic vinegar, pinch of salt and pepper. Sauté the chopped onion in the olive oil till soft, about 3–5 minutes. Cool.

With your hands mix the cooled onion into the meat mixture, wet your hand in cold water and shape the meat mixture into 6 large or 12 small hamburgers . . . You can freeze them at this stage, if you like, or you can put them on a plastic tray or board and cover them with clingfilm and keep them in the fridge till you are ready to cook. Take them from the fridge into room temperature about an hour before grilling them. Grill them for about 3–4 minutes, turning them over so that they cook evenly.

Special Occasion Lunches

SPECIAL OCCASION LUNCHES

There are occasions, for any age group, when a celebration forms a lunch party rather than an evening party. Whether it is to celebrate a birthday, anniversary, graduation, wedding – whatever, a lunch-time party will often be the occasion chosen for a variety of reasons. There are two chief reasons, above all others, and they are that some of the guests may have to travel some distance and this is easiest done in the day-time, and the other, and most important, is that when people are older they much prefer to eat on a more expansive scale in the middle of the day rather than in the evening.

A special occasion lunch calls for a first course, a main course and a pud. In this chapter there are some first course suggestions and some main course ideas, and the puddings can be chosen from the chapter composed entirely of pudding recipes. But in the chapter on Business Lunches you will find some dishes which are ideally suited to be first courses, on a slightly scaled-down basis. And other chapters, most notably the one on Sunday Lunches, contain main courses eminently suitable for this chapter, too. So look through the book and adapt recipes as they appeal to you.

Marinated Kipper Fillets in Lime

Quails' Egg and Smoked Salmon Salad with Dill Dressing

Marinated Grilled Aubergines

Parmesan Croûtons

Avocado and Tomato Pâté

Marinated Mushrooms

Asparagus Mousse

FIRST COURSE SUGGESTIONS

For a first course, the seasons will dictate to a great extent what you decide to give your guests. If the weather is chilly, you may prefer to give them a hot first course, but as a general rule-of-thumb a cold first course is much easier for the cook, and in this chapter all the suggestions are cold, for convenience. Seasonally speaking, a simple salad of steamed asparagus is hard to beat, but that hardly constitutes a recipe! Smoked salmon, or Gravad Lax, are also delicious first courses, and nothing could be simpler than either. But if you want to give your guests a simple smoked fish first course that is a bit more unusual, give them smoked eel; it is, to my mind, the best of all smoked fish. I buy our smoked eel from the Achiltibuie Smoke House, at the Summer Isles.

Marinated Kipper Fillets in Lime

Too many recipes go in fashions of usefulness. Marinated kipper fillets are such a dish, and yet what a waste of a good recipe! It is one of the most convenient and delicious first courses, and not at all difficult or time-consuming to make. I like to use the distinctive flavour of limes in the marinade – we can even buy limes in the Co-op in Broadford, Skye, so I would think they are obtainable in all parts of rural Britain, too!

SERVES 6

---

6 plump kippers
¼ pt/140 ml extra virgin
   olive oil
3 limes, well washed and
   dried to remove their
   preservative, then the
   rinds finely grated and
   the juices squeezed

1 tsp grainy mustard –
   either Moutarde de
   Meaux, or Isabella's
   Mustard Relish, from
   Ellon in Aberdeenshire
1–2 tbsp finely chopped
   parsley and snipped
   chives, mixed

Put each kipper on a board. With a very sharp knife slice the kipper flesh from the bones and skin. You will inevitably get some shredded looking bits of kipper but it doesn't matter – it's impossible not to. Slice the bigger bits of kipper flesh into thin strips and put them into a shallow dish.

Mix together the olive oil, lime rinds and juices, mustard and chopped parsley and chives and pour this over the strips of kipper, mixing it in well – I find a fork easiest to use for this. Cover the dish, and leave in a cool place to marinate for at least 24 hours, forking the marinade through the kipper strips two or three times during the marinating.

Serve on individual plates with a small heap of salad and brown bread and butter.

Quails' Eggs and Smoked Salmon Salad with Dill Dressing

Quails' eggs are easy to buy these days, and I love them. They have a creamier taste than hens' eggs, and they look so attractive. A few extra quails' eggs, with only the top part of their shells removed, look very decorative scattered about as a garnish. Or if you choose to arrange the salad on individual serving plates, one half-shelled egg will be all the garnish needed.

SERVES 6

Assorted lettuce leaves
18 quails' eggs, boiled for 3
   minutes, then run under
   cold water
½ lb/225 g smoked salmon,
   sliced into thin strips

For the dressing:
5 tbsp extra virgin olive oil
1 tbsp white wine vinegar,
   or 1 tsp balsamic vinegar
A handful of dill fronds
1 tsp Dijon mustard
½ tsp caster sugar
½ tsp salt and a good
   grinding of black pepper

You can either arrange this simple salad first course on a serving plate, or on individual plates. Arrange the lettuce leaves, which can consist of a variety such as lollo rosso, oak leaved lettuce, rocket, baby spinach – anything you choose or can get. Shell twelve of the eggs, and cut each one in half. Put a small tangled heap of strips of smoked salmon in the middle of each plate, or, if you are using one serving plate, down the centre. Arrange the halved eggs around, and half shell the remaining six eggs, as described in the introduction to this recipe, and put one on each plate, or dot them around the outer edges of the lettuce on the big serving plate.

Put all the ingredients for the dressing into a liquidizer and whiz till smooth. Pour this around the egg and lettuce of the salad, leaving the smoked salmon glistening in the middle.

Marinated Grilled Aubergines

I love aubergines, and I ate the most delicious marinated aubergines last November in a small restaurant in a tiny back street in the middle of Rome. We went back to the same restaurant in February and the same marinated aubergines were again part of the excellent antipasto served as a first course. This is how I reconstructed them.

SERVES 6

3 fairly large, firm
aubergines – more if they
are small
Salt
Olive oil
For the marinade:
³/₄ pt/420 ml of the best
extra virgin olive oil
2 cloves of garlic, poached
in their skins for

1 minute, then skinned
and chopped finely
A handful of parsley,
chopped quite fine
¹/₂ tsp salt and plenty of
freshly ground black
pepper
A sprig of fresh thyme, the
tiny leaves stripped from
the stalks

Slice off both ends of the aubergines. Slice the aubergines lengthways about ¼ inch/5 mm thick and sprinkle the slices with salt. Leave till little beads of dark liquid bubble up then wipe them dry with absorbent paper. Brush each slice on either side with olive oil then grill or – nicest – barbecue the slices, or fry them, till they are tender. This doesn't take a minute once you have turned them as they cook.

Mix together the marinade ingredients. As the aubergines slices are cooked, put them on to a large serving plate or ashet. Pour the marinade over them and leave for several hours, or overnight.

These are delicious served with the Black Olive, Sun-Dried Tomato and Garlic Bread on page 68.

Parmesan Croûtons

These puff up as they bake, and I like to serve them with a small heap of dressed salad. Although their cooking is last-minute, all the preparation can be done well in advance – you can make the simple Parmesan mixture the day before. This recipe was given to me by my American Aunt Janie, at whose house in Connecticut I first ate these.

SERVES 6

---

6 slices, about ⅓ inch/1 cm thick, cut, if possible, from a baked white loaf	*2 tsp very finely chopped red onion (this is about half an onion)*
6 oz/170 g freshly grated Parmesan cheese	*A pinch of salt and a good grinding of black pepper*
½ pt/285 ml good mayonnaise	

If you like – I do because it looks better – trim each slice of bread into a round about 3 inches/7.5 cm in diameter. Toast lightly on each side – just till pale golden.

Mix the Parmesan with the mayonnaise, onion and seasoning,

and divide it between the pieces of toast. Smooth the mixture over each piece so that it comes right up to the edges.

Bake in a moderate oven, 350°F/180°C/Gas Mark 4, for 20–25 minutes, till the croûtons are golden brown and puffed up. Serve as soon as you can, with dressed mixed green salad.

Avocado and Tomato Pâté

This is my version of guacamole. I like it much better than any I have either bought in a supermarket or eaten in a restaurant and I have come to the conclusion that there are two things I don't like in guacamole: raw onion, in however infinitesimal amounts, and mayonnaise. Now, I can hear people saying that a true guacamole doesn't have mayonnaise in, but several versions do, and the combination of avocado and mayonnaise is, to me, soapy. This is such a simple and useful pâté – you can either serve it as a first course, or as a dip – and I like the crème fraîche which to my taste cuts the denseness of the avocado as well as greatly complementing the flavour, and the chopped tomatoes. I use snipped chives instead of chopped onions.

SERVES 6

3 good ripe avocados – it's always better to buy 4, because you can never tell whether one may be fibrous inside.

2 tsp lemon juice

2 tubs of crème fraîche (7 fl oz/200 ml each)

3 tomatoes, each skinned,

cut in half and de-seeded, and the tomatoes chopped into neat dice

About 1 tbsp snipped chives

A good dash of Tabasco sauce

Salt and pepper to your taste

Cut the avocados in half and scoop their flesh into a food processor. Add the lemon juice and whiz to a smooth purée. Add the crème fraîche and briefly whiz, just enough to combine everything. Scrape this mixture into a bowl, and stir in the diced tomatoes, the snipped chives, Tabasco, salt and pepper. Cover the bowl with clingfilm and leave it in the fridge till you are ready to dish up.

Arrange a small heap of salad leaves on serving plates and put a mound of the avocado and tomato pâté in the middle of each. Do this as near to eating as you can, to let the avocado discolour as little as possible.

Marinated Mushrooms

It sounds rather a lot of mushrooms in this recipe, I realize, but they do go down so much as they cook. It is worthwhile cooking the mushrooms in the olive oil till they are crisp – their flavour is very much better. This is a tip passed on to me by Brigadier Ley, one of the best cooks I know, and such a source of inspiration and culinary know-how. You may need more olive oil to sauté the mushrooms than I say – this depends on your sauté pan; a non-stick pan will need less oil than a non non-stick one! This is awfully good.

SERVES 6

2 lbs/900 g mushrooms, each wiped, stalks trimmed level with the caps and the mushrooms sliced quite thickly

5–6 tbsp olive oil – don't add it to the sauté pan all at the beginning, start with 3 tbsp and add more as you need it

For the marinade:

4 tbsp extra virgin olive oil

1 – 2 cloves of garlic, skinned and chopped finely

½ pt/285 ml chicken (or vegetable) stock

¼ pt/140 ml dry white wine

½ tsp dried thyme or a good sprig of fresh, tiny leaves stripped from it

Salt and pepper

3 tomatoes, skinned, cut in half and de-seeded, and the tomatoes finely diced

Torn-up basil leaves

Cook the sliced mushrooms in relays, in a sauté pan with the olive oil. Cook them till they are almost crisp, then remove them to a shallow, wide serving dish. As they are sautéing, make the marinade.

Into a wide shallow pan put the olive oil, chopped garlic, stock and white wine, thyme, salt and pepper. Bring to simmering point and simmer gently for 5 minutes. Take it off the heat and leave to cool completely. Then stir in the diced tomatoes and the torn-up basil. Pour this over the sautéed mushrooms and leave overnight in a cool larder or the fridge.

I like to arrange the marinated mushrooms on plates, spooned, with the marinade, over lettuce leaves. Accompany, if you like, with warm bread or with the Sesame Toasts on page 71.

Asparagus Mousse

This is easy and delicious. If you like, you can make it in ramekins and turn out each mousse on individual serving plates. Serve it with either a small heap of steamed asparagus at the side, or with a tangled small heap of strips of smoked salmon or eel, or with a small amount of dressed salad leaves.

SERVES 6

---

¹⁄₄ pt/140 ml good chicken stock or vegetable stock
1 sachet of powdered gelatine
1 lb/450 g asparagus, steamed or microwaved till just tender when you stick a fork into the

thickest part of each stem, then with cold water run through to refresh its colour
Salt and pepper
A grating of nutmeg
2 pots of crème fraîche (7 fl oz/200 ml each)
2 egg whites

Put the stock into a small saucepan and heat it, then sprinkle the gelatine over it. Shake the pan, taking care not to let the liquid boil, till the gelatine dissolves completely and you can see no granules. Let this cool.

Put the cooked asparagus into a processor and whiz till as smooth as you can. Whiz in the stock and gelatine mixture, then push this through a sieve, for the smoothest texture. (This depends how sharp the blades of your processor are!) Season the purée with salt and pepper, and a grating of nutmeg. Fold the crème fraîche through the purée.

In a bowl, whisk the egg whites till very stiff, then, with a large metal spoon, fold them quickly and thoroughly through the purée. Pour the mousse mixture into a serving bowl, cover, and leave to set in a cool place, a fridge or larder.

If you want to set it in ramekins, rub each out with a very small amount of oil – I use sunflower for this – before putting the mousse mixture in. To turn them out, I run a knife around the inside of the ramekins, and the contents should then turn out easily. This can be made a day in advance.

Oxtail Stew

Silverside of Beef with Root Vegetables, Dumplings and Horseradish Dressing

Leg of Lamb with Lemon and Caper Sauce

Roast Loin of Pork with Leeks, Apples and Cream

Braised Lamb Cutlets with Redcurrant Jelly and Red Wine

Pheasant Casseroled with Bacon, Shallots and Mushrooms

Monkfish in Saffron Cream Sauce

MAIN COURSES

There are very many subjects suitable for a special main course in other chapters in this book, most notably in the Sunday Lunches chapter. What you decide to give your guests for the special occasion will be dictated by who the guests are – if they are elderly and live alone or in a couple, any roast meat will be a treat because elderly people and those who live in small households very rarely bother to buy something sufficiently large to merit roasting. In this chapter there are recipes for old British dishes which we tend to forget about, such as Silverside of Beef with Root Vegetables, Dumplings and Horseradish Dressing, or Leg of Lamb with Lemon and Caper Sauce. The Braised Lamb Cutlets with Redcurrant Jelly and Red Wine are very good – my sister Camilla makes this dish and I love it. The Pheasant Casseroled with Bacon, Shallots and Mushrooms is both convenient and delicious. And for warmer weather, or for those who don't eat meat, there is the Monkfish in Saffron Cream Sauce.

Oxtail Stew

To my mind, this is the best casserole of any meat. An oxtail has to be cooked long and slowly, and as with all casseroles this benefits greatly from being cooked and reheated. This allows you to skim off any excess fat when it has cooled after its first cooking, and it also lets the flavours of the meat and vegetables mingle together. An Oxtail Stew is a rich and deeply satisfying dish, and absolutely perfect for a special occasion main course on a chilly winter's day. Beware, though, of ever buying a frozen oxtail. They are horrible – why oxtails don't freeze successfully raw I don't know, they are the only cut of meat I can think of which doesn't freeze well. But when it is cooked, it freezes as well as any other casserole or stew.

SERVES 6

2 oxtails (any left over can either be reheated and eaten up, or made into soup)	Half a turnip, peeled and diced neatly
	1 clove of garlic, skinned and chopped finely
4 tbsp olive or sunflower oil	2 fairly level tbsp flour
3 medium-sized onions, each skinned and finely chopped	2 tbsp tomato pureé
	1 can of lager + 1–1½ pts/ 570–850 ml water
3 carrots, peeled and chopped neatly	Salt and pepper

With a very sharp knife (which will make the task quicker), trim as much fat and gristle off each piece of oxtail as you can. Heat the oil in a heavy casserole and brown each piece of oxtail all over, removing the pieces to a warm dish as they are browned. Lower the heat a bit under the casserole and sauté the chopped onions for several minutes, stirring occasionally, until they are really soft and beginning to turn golden at the edges. Then stir in the chopped carrots and turnip, and the garlic. Cook for a couple of minutes, then stir in the flour and cook for a further couple of minutes. Stir in the tomato pureé, lager and 1 pint/570 ml of the water, stirring till the liquid begins to bubble gently. Then season with salt and pepper and replace the pieces of browned oxtail in the casserole, pushing them down amongst the vegetables in the sauce.

Cover the casserole with its lid and cook in a fairly low temperature oven, 250°F/120°C/Gas Mark ½, for 3 hours. Take it out of the oven and let it cool completely – store it in a cool place like a larder or fridge. Skim any fat from the surface.

Reheat by taking the casserole out of the fridge and into room temperature for an hour before putting it into the oven, this time a moderate oven, 350°F/180°C/Gas Mark 4, for 2 hours. Check the liquid and stir in a bit more water as it cooks if you think it is needed. If you put the casserole straight from the fridge into the oven, add 30 minutes on to the reheating and cooking time.

I like to serve this with very creamily mashed and beaten potatoes, and the vegetables which I like best with oxtail are either cabbage or spring greens.

Silverside of Beef with Root Vegetables, Dumplings and Horseradish Dressing

Silverside is a lean meat, unlike the much fattier brisket, which could be used for this dish instead of the silverside. But I prefer the silverside because of its leanness. The vegetable content of this dish is quite enough – there is no need to have any other vegetable accompaniment. The Horseradish Dressing is best made with creamy Moniack horseradish, far and away the best horseradish sauce to be bought.

SERVES 6 (ANY LEFT OVER CAN BE REHEATED OR MADE INTO SOUP)

3 lb/1.3 kg rolled silverside
Cold water to cover the
* meat – about 4 pts/2.3 l*
6 onions, skinned
6 carrots, trimmed, peeled
* and left whole*
About half a turnip, peeled
* and sliced in neat strips*
6 potatoes, peeled and left
whole – try and use
* potatoes of as near the*
* same size as you can*
3 large parsnips, trimmed,
* peeled and each cut in*
* half lengthwise*
6 leeks, washed and
* trimmed to the same*
* length*
Salt and pepper

Put the meat into a large casserole and cover with cold water. Over a moderate heat bring the water slowly to the boil – this should not be hurried. Skim off, with a metal spoon, any scum which forms on the water. The water should take 25–30 minutes to reach a gentle bubble. Put the onions, carrots and turnip into the casserole with the meat and simmer all very gently for an hour, skimming the surface clean as it is needed. Then add the potatoes, parsnips and leeks, season with salt and pepper and cook gently for a further 30 minutes. Then add the dumplings.

Dumplings

8 oz/225 g self raising flour	*4 oz/112 g shredded suet*
Salt and pepper	*Finely grated rind of 1 lemon*

Sieve the flour, salt and pepper together and mix with the suet and grated lemon rind. Mix in just enough cold water to form a dough, and, with floured hands, form the dumplings into small balls about the size of a ping-pong ball. Drop them into the simmering liquid, amongst the vegetables, and simmer for a further 20–25 minutes cooking.

Lift the meat from the casserole and on to a warmed serving plate. It should be very tender. Carve, and serve with the vegetables and dumplings.

Horseradish Dressing

½ pt/285 ml of the best horseradish sauce you can find	*1 tub of crème fraîche (7 fl oz/200 ml)*

Mix together well, and serve in a separate bowl.

Leg of Lamb with Lemon and Caper Sauce

One of the classic British dishes is boiled leg of mutton with caper sauce. Well, it is almost impossible to buy mutton these days, and I don't much care for the flavour of lamb or mutton on the leg when it is boiled, but this dish is my version of the classic. The lamb we buy is several months old – a leg weighs about 7 pounds/3 kilos – and as I don't care for baby anything (except vegetables) I think our lamb has superb flavour. It is hard to find lamb in the world better in flavour than that raised in the Highlands and Islands. As taste develops with maturity we have the tender succulent meat as well as extremely good flavour.

In this recipe the lamb is baked in a deep roasting tin with vegetables around it and the joint half submerged in liquid. The sauce is made from some of the strained liquid (make the rest into soup with the vegetables), thickened with a small amount of flour, egg yolks and cream, and flavoured with lemon. For the caper content it is worthwhile seeking out the very best capers you can find – they are a world apart from the run-of-the-mill capers tasting of nothing but the harsh brine in which they are preserved.

SERVES 6–8

---

1 leg of lamb weighing 6–7 lb/2.5–3 kg
Butter
½ pt/285 ml red wine and 2 pt/1.1 l water
3 onions, skinned and cut in half
3 carrots, trimmed and chopped
3 sticks of celery, washed, trimmed and chopped
3 leeks, washed, trimmed and chopped
A sprig of rosemary
For the sauce:
2 oz/56 g butter

2 oz/56 g flour
1 pt/570 ml strained stock from around the cooked meat
3 oz/84 g butter, cut into bits
Grated rind of 1 lemon and its juice
¼ pt/140 ml double cream
Freshly ground black pepper – taste to see if salt is needed and add it as you like
4 tsp of the best capers you can buy – a good delicatessen should stock salted capers

---

Trim any excess fat from the lamb and rub it with a small amount of butter. Put it into a deep roasting tin with the wine and water, the vegetables and the rosemary. Put the tin into a hot oven, 400°F/ 200°C/Gas Mark 6, and cook for 2 hours, basting the meat at regular intervals with the liquid. Halfway through the cooking time put a piece of greaseproof paper or a couple of butter papers over the top of the meat. If you prefer less well done meat, give the meat less cooking time – this will give you very slightly pink meat. Lift the meat, once cooked, on to a warmed serving plate. Strain 1 pint/570 ml of the stock from around the meat.

Make the sauce by melting the butter in a saucepan and stirring in the flour. Let it cook for a minute then, stirring continuously – I find a small balloon whisk ideal for this and all sauce-making – add the stock. Stir till the sauce boils. Take the pan off the heat and whisk in the bits of butter, a piece at a time. Whisk in the lemon rind and juice and lastly, the cream. Season with pepper, add the capers and mix them well into the sauce, then check to see if you think it is sufficiently salty.

Keep the sauce warm as you carve the meat, and serve it separately. This lamb is nicest, I think, with barely steamed sugar snap peas.

Roast Loin of Pork with Leeks, Apples and Cream

Anyone who doesn't like mustard need have no fear about the mustard content in the sauce – you don't notice it as such, I promise you.

SERVES 6–8

A 4–5 lb/1.8–2.2 kg loin of	*trimmed and sliced about*
pork, boned	*2 inches/5 cm thick*
4 good-sized leeks, washed,	*4 eating apples, e.g. Cox's –*

not dreary Golden	*2 tsp Dijon mustard*
Delicious, which aren't a	*1 pt/570 ml water and dry*
bit – peeled, cored and	*white wine mixed*
cut in chunks	*½ pt/285 ml single cream*
	Salt and pepper

Put the loin into a roasting tin and into a hot oven, 425°F/220°C/ Gas Mark 7, for 20 minutes. Then take it out of the oven and put the leeks and apples into the roasting tin with the pork on top. Mix the mustard into the water and wine and pour that into the roasting tin. Put the tin back into the hot oven and cook for a further 30 minutes. Then fork around the leeks and apples so that any at the outer edges in the liquid don't singe, and continue to cook so that the meat has in total 20 minutes per pound/450 g with about 15 minutes over. Keep an eye on the meat and cover its surface with a butter paper if it looks as if it is browning too much. Take the meat out of the roasting tin and put it on a serving plate in a warm oven whilst you make the sauce.

Pour and scrape the contents of the roasting tin into a food processor and whiz to a smooth purée, gradually adding the cream. Taste, and add salt and pepper to the extent you like. Reheat this sauce carefully, so as not to let it simmer, and serve it with the sliced roast pork.

To me, this cries out for a crisp green vegetable, such as barely steamed sugar snap peas, and for mashed potatoes, to go with it.

Braised Lamb Cutlets with Redcurrant Jelly and Red Wine

These are simple to make, good to eat, and convenient in that they can be prepared and baked well in advance of your guests arriving and covered and kept warm in a low temperature oven. I like to serve them with very well and creamily mashed potatoes and with leeks in a nutmeg-flavoured creamy sauce. Sautéed parsnips are another delicious and complementary accompaniment.

About 3 tbsp oil – I use sunflower for this	*1 bottle of red wine, I use a Beaujolais for this*
2 onions, skinned and sliced very thinly	*2 tsp redcurrant jelly – homemade if at all possible, it has a so much better taste*
12 lamb cutlets – more, if your guests have large appetites	*Salt and freshly ground black pepper*

In a wide sauté pan heat the oil and sauté the sliced onions till they are just turning golden at their edges. Scoop them into a wide ovenproof dish. Brown the cutlets on both sides and put them, as they brown, on to the onions. Pour the wine into the sauté pan and stir in the redcurrant jelly. Let this bubble for a couple of minutes, and the jelly melt in the wine. Season with salt and pepper and pour this over the chops.

Cover the surface of the chops with greaseproof paper or with butter papers, and bake in a moderate oven, 350°F/180°C/Gas Mark 4, for 40 minutes. The wine will reduce as the cutlets cook.

Then keep the dish warm in a very low temperature oven till you are ready to eat.

Pheasant Casseroled with Bacon, Shallots and Mushrooms

This is really like coq au vin only with pheasant instead of chicken. I think it is an awfully good way to use pheasant, which tends to dryness in cooking if you're not careful. Pheasants are widely available in city supermarkets and butchers these days, and their flavour is very mildly gamey. This is a most delicious casserole, full of richly complementary flavours.

SERVES 6–8

2 fairly small pheasants	*with the caps, and the*
4 tbsp olive oil	*mushrooms quartered*
1 lb/450 g shallots, skinned	*1 level tsp flour*
6 slices of the best back	*1 bottle of red wine, ideally*
bacon you can buy,	*a Beaujolais*
trimmed of fat	*Salt and pepper*
1 lb/450 g mushrooms, each	*2 bayleaves*
wiped, stalks cut level	

Pull out any fat from inside each pheasant. Heat the oil in a heavy casserole and brown the pheasants all over in the hot oil. As they are browned, put them on to a warm dish. Then add the skinned shallots to the casserole, and cook them gently, shaking the casserole so that they brown all over. Meanwhile slice the bacon into thin strips and add those to the shallots. Cook for several minutes, then, with a large slotted spoon, remove the shallots and bacon to the dish with the pheasants.

Turn up the heat under the casserole and sauté the chopped mushrooms till they are almost crisp – this much improves their flavour. Turn the heat back down to moderate, stir in the flour and cook for a moment, then pour in the wine, stirring till the sauce bubbles. Season with salt and pepper. Replace the shallots and bacon in the casserole, and the pheasants, pushing them down amongst the vegetables and bacon. Tuck in the bayleaves.

Cover the casserole with its lid and cook in a moderate oven, 350°F/180°C/Gas Mark 4, for 1 hour. Stick the point of a sharp knife into the thigh of one of the pheasants – if the juices run clear, take the casserole out of the oven. Carve the birds, replacing the pheasant meat in amongst the bacon, shallots and mushrooms in their winey sauce. Keep the carcases and make stock with them.

Gently reheat to serve. Either very creamily mashed potatoes, or crisp sautéed potatoes with paprika, are good with this. Or you could – Godfrey would! – have plain boiled Basmati rice. Any green vegetable, such as broccoli or spring greens, goes very well with the pheasant casserole. And it freezes beautifully.

You can make it in advance by a day or two (provided you keep it in a cool place, like the fridge), reheating it till it bubbles very gently – fast boiling spoils the texture of the ingredients and will render the cooked pheasant shredded – for 10 minutes before serving.

Monkfish in Saffron Cream Sauce

I blush when I think back 23 years, when we first began to run Kinloch, our home, as a hotel. I had never even heard of monkfish then – my only consolation is that neither had most other people, because monkfish, for the most part, used to be thrown back by the fishermen, in those far-off days, with the exception of the less than scrupulous who used to buy it, dip it in breadcrumbs and freeze it, and pass it off as scampi tails. That gives you an idea of the texture of monkfish – it is a robust fish, and now fetches a very high price in the fish markets. It is much sought after, and I prize it highly for its versatility. Here it is in a rich and delicious sauce, flavoured with that aromatic spice saffron, the most exotic of all spices – and the most expensive. It is is only worth buying the strands of saffron, the powdered stuff is adulterated and bulked up by other powder than pulverized saffron. Saffron complements the flavour of fish and shellfish.

SERVES 6

---

1 pt/570 ml fish stock	*1½ lb/675 g trimmed*
2 oz/56 g butter	*monkfish tails, each cut*
2 onions, skinned and very	*into bits about 1 inch/2.5*
finely chopped	*cm long*
2 good pinches saffron	*Salt and pepper*
½ pt/285 ml double cream	

Fish stock can be bought in some supermarkets if you don't make your own, although if you have a microwave you can do this in 25 minutes by putting fish bones and skin, any chopped vegetables, and crushed parsley stalks into a bowl of water, to cook in your microwave on medium high setting. It is so easy.

In a good wide and heavy-based sauté pan, melt the butter and cook the chopped onions for several minutes – till they are soft and beginning to turn golden. Pour in the stock, and let this simmer, with the saffron stirred in, till it has reduced by about two-thirds, then stir in the cream. Stir in the chopped monkfish at this stage, too, and let the cream bubble – the sauce will thicken as the cream boils, and have no fear of it curdling, it won't if the cream is double rather than single. In the 2–3 minutes that the sauce bubbles the monkfish will cook – stir it all around gently, so that it cooks evenly. Taste, and season with salt and pepper to your liking. The sauce will have the rich golden hue of saffron.

This is nicest served with rice, which I like to stir chopped parsley through just before serving, to make its appearance more interesting. Sugar snap peas are my ideal vegetable accompaniment – particularly if they are sliced and stir-fried with grated ginger.

Lunch-Time Puddings

Rhubarb and Ginger Fudge Crumble

Lemon and Syrup Sponge with Vanilla Custard

Apple and Fudge Gingerbread Pudding

Orange, Grape and Ginger Terrine

Coffee and Chipped Dark Chocolate Ice Cream with Warm Caramel Sauce

Date and Ginger Pudding

Lemon Roulade with Raspberry Cream

Tarte aux Fruits

Poached Pears with Ginger Crème Anglaise

Blackberry (or Raspberry) and Lemon Mousse Cake

Strawberry and Cinnamon Meringue Bombe

Chocolate and Ginger Meringue Bombe

Dark Chocolate Soufflés

Lemon and Vanilla Soufflés

Pear and Almond Glazed Tarts

Baked Nectarine, Raspberry and Cinnamon Pudding

Puffed Chocolate Chip and Pecan Biscuits·

Lime and Mango Sorbet with Mango Salad and Lime

Bread and Butter Pudding with Cream and Nutmeg

Fudge Brownie Pie with Vanilla Ice Cream

Lemon Crumble Cake

LUNCH-TIME PUDDINGS

The recipes in this chapter are, of course, suitable for eating at dinner-time as well as at lunch-time! I do love making and eating puddings (sadly) and in this chapter is the collection of recipes which I have accumulated since I last wrote anything sweet. The best part about the life I lead is the fact that when you have to cook for the hotel guests, as I do, with Peter Macpherson and Claire Munro, there is the endless potential for invention, and for variations on themes of puddings.

In this chapter there are recipes for warming, everyday types of pudding, such as the Rhubarb and Ginger Fudge Crumble, and the Apple and Fudge Gingerbread Pudding. There are easy and convenient recipes suitable for entertaining, such as the two bombes: the Strawberry and Cinnamon Meringue Bombe and the Chocolate and Ginger Meringue Bombe. There are a couple of recipes for sweet soufflés – these are so much easier and more convenient than many people imagine a soufflé to be. There are recipes for summery puds, such as the Orange, Grape and Ginger Terrine, and the Lime and Mango Sorbet with Mango Salad and Lime. I hope there will be ideas within this chapter to tempt others with teeth as sweet as my own!

Rhubarb and Ginger Fudge Crumble

I prefer to cook food in its natural season, and yet this pud can be made at any time of the year because rhubarb freezes so very well. Simply cut in chunks and pack into polythene bags.

Rhubarb combines well with orange, ginger and cinnamon, and in this recipe you find the first two. It is a convenient pud in that the rhubarb can be baked a day (or even two) in advance, and the pudding can be made, with its crumbly fudgy top, and reheated – I do prefer to serve it warm. You can accompany it either with thick natural yoghurt, or with crème fraîche, or with good vanilla ice cream, whichever you prefer.

SERVES 6–8

1½ lb/675 g rhubarb, washed and trimmed and cut into chunks – and weighed after trimming

4 oz/112 g soft light or dark brown sugar, or 4 tbsp honey

Finely grated rind of 2 oranges – wash (and dry)

them well before using the rind

For the topping:

4 oz/112 g butter

4 oz/112 g demerara sugar

2 tsp powdered ginger

8 oz/225 g digestive biscuits, crushed or whizzed to crumbs

½ tsp vanilla essence

Put the cut-up rhubarb into a Pyrex dish with the sugar and orange rind. Cover the dish and bake in a moderate oven, 350°F/180°C/ Gas Mark 4, till the pieces of rhubarb are tender. As the rhubarb cooks juice will seep from it – don't be tempted to add water to the rhubarb because you will end up with far too much liquid amongst the pieces of rhubarb. Take the dish out of the oven and cool it.

Melt the butter in a saucepan, and stir in the demerara sugar. Stir in the ginger and the biscuit crumbs, and, if you like, the vanilla essence. Mix this very well, then spoon it over the top of the cooled rhubarb. Bake in a moderate oven for 20–25 minutes, until firm on top

Lemon and Syrup Sponge with Vanilla Custard

There is nothing to beat a hot pudding on a chilly day. But puddings such as this steamed Lemon and Syrup Sponge are so much better eaten at lunch-time than in the evening for dinner or supper, when they can lie rather heavily on the tum – I prefer to give lighter puddings in the evening. Some people tend to think

that steamed puddings are laborious to make and rather compli-
cated – nothing could be farther from the truth. The lemon in this
recipe tends to taste like lemon marmalade after the length of
cooking, but that is the taste I love.

SERVES 6

*4 generous tbsp golden
    syrup – if you dip the
    spoon in very hot water
    before each spoonful, the
    syrup will slip easily off
    the spoon
Finely grated rind of 3
    lemons – wash them well
    first, and dry them
8 oz/225 g self-raising flour
1 tsp bicarbonate of soda*

*A pinch of salt
4 oz/112 g grated or
    shredded suet – use
    vegetarian suet if you
    prefer
3 oz/84 g soft light brown
    sugar
1 large egg
¼ pt/140 ml milk
1 tsp vanilla essence, or a
    few drops of vanilla
    extract*

You will need a 3–4 pint/1.7–2.3 litre boilable plastic pudding bowl
with a snap-on lid. There is no need to grease or butter this, but you
will need to if you are using any other type of bowl to steam your
pud in.

Start by spooning the syrup into the bottom of the pudding bowl,
and mix about a quarter of the grated lemon rind in with the syrup.
Sieve the flour, bicarbonate of soda and salt into a bowl. Stir in the
suet, sugar, egg, milk, vanilla and the rest of the grated lemon rind,
mixing all together very well. Spoon and scrape this on top of the
syrup.

Cut a disc of parchment to cover the top of the pudding, but
make a pleat in the centre of the paper to allow for the pudding to
rise up slightly as it cooks. Put this paper over the surface of the
pudding. Snap on the lid of the pudding bowl, and put the bowl
into a large saucepan with water coming halfway up the sides of the
bowl. Simmer the water around the pudding bowl for 2½–3 hours,
with the lid on the pan. Check the level of the water from time to

time, so that it runs no risk of simmering dry. Top it up when necessary.

Before serving, if you like, turn the pudding out on to a warmed plate, otherwise just spoon it straight from the bowl. Serve with Vanilla Custard, if you like – I do!

Vanilla Custard

4 large egg yolks	½ tsp vanilla essence, or a
3 oz/84g caster sugar	few drops of extract
1 level tsp cornflour, sieved	1 pint/570 ml milk or, better
	still, single cream

Beat together the yolks, sugar, cornflour and vanilla, gradually mixing in the milk (or cream). Either cook by stirring, in a heavy-based saucepan, over a gentle heat till the custard thickens – this is a lengthy process and can't be hurried for fear of curdling the custard; or, if you have a microwave, put the bowl into the microwave on a halfway heat setting for 2 minutes. Take out and whisk the custard, then replace it in the microwave for a further 2 minutes on halfway heat. Whisk, and repeat the cooking – it will take between 6 and 8 minutes' cooking altogether to thicken. Serve warm.

Apple and Fudge Gingerbread Pudding

Here is another perfect winter pudding. Nothing is so comforting as a good pudding for lunch on a chilly day. This pudding can be made in a foil dish and frozen, then reheated before turning out to serve. You can accompany it with the Vanilla Custard in the previous recipe or with crème fraîche, or natural yoghurt, or good vanilla ice cream.

For the base of the pudding – which becomes the top when the pudding is turned out to serve:	For the gingerbread:
2 oz/56 g butter	*4 oz/112 g self-raising flour*
4 oz/112 g soft brown sugar	*½ tsp bicarbonate of soda*
3 good eating apples, e.g. Cox's, peeled, quartered, cored and each quarter sliced as thinly as possible	*2 tsp powdered cinnamon*
	A grating of nutmeg
	2 tsp ground ginger
	Grated rind of 1 lemon and 1 orange
Chopped ginger, drained of its syrup (optional)	*1 large egg*
	4 oz/112 g soft brown sugar
	3 oz/84 g treacle
	4 fl oz/112 ml milk (just less than ¼ pint)
	2 oz/56 g butter, melted

Melt the butter and dissolve the sugar together in a saucepan over moderate heat. Stir for a couple of minutes while it bubbles gently once the sugar has dissolved completely. Pour into an ovenproof dish (9″ × 4″/23 × 10 cm). Arrange the thinly sliced apples over the base of the dish, on top of the butter and sugar mixture, and scatter on the chopped ginger if used.

Make the gingerbread by sieving together the flour, bicarbonate of soda, cinnamon, nutmeg and ginger into a bowl. Add the grated orange and lemon rinds. Mix together the egg, sugar, treacle, milk and melted butter, mixing all this into the sieved contents of the bowl. Mix all together very well, then pour and scrape this over the apples. Smooth it even, and bake in a moderate oven, 350°F/ 180°C/Gas Mark 4, for 40–45 minutes till firm to the touch. Serve warm.

Orange, Grape and Ginger Terrine

This is one of my favourite puddings at any time of the year. Many supermarkets stock fresh orange juice in convenient pint-sized bottles for using when you can't be bothered to squeeze your own. This a perfect pud to end an otherwise rather heavy and/ or rich lunch.

SERVES 8

½ pt/285 ml orange liqueur and water mixed – I leave the ratio up to you!
juice of half a lemon
2 oz/56 g caster sugar
2 sachets of powdered gelatine (1 oz/28 g) or 8 leaves of gelatine

1 pt/570 ml fresh orange juice
¾ lb/340 g grapes, green or black, cut in half and seeds removed
6–8 pieces of preserved ginger, drained of their syrup and chopped neatly

Line a 2 lb/900 g loaf tin with clingfilm.

Put the ½ pint/285 ml orange liqueur and water, the lemon juice and the caster sugar into a saucepan over a moderate heat and stir till the sugar has dissolved. Then either sprinkle in the gelatine or feed in the gelatine leaves, whichever you are using – the leaves are the best to use. Stir till the gelatine is dissolved but don't let the liquid boil. Take the pan off the heat and cool. Then stir it into the fresh orange juice. Stir the halved de-seeded grapes into the liquid, along with the chopped ginger, and pour it into the lined loaf tin. Leave to set in the fridge, forking through the contents of the loaf tin to make sure that the grapes don't sink to the bottom as it sets but are distributed as evenly as possible.

If you like, serve a compote of sliced oranges scattered with chips of caramel to go with the terrine. Turn it out by dipping the tin briefly in hot water – not too hot as otherwise it melts the jelly – turn it upside down on to a serving plate, peel off the clingfilm, dip a knife in a jug of hot water and slice to serve.

Coffee and Chipped Dark Chocolate Ice Cream with Warm Caramel Sauce

The inspiration for this ice cream came when I was indulging in a visit to Häagen Dazs, in Heathrow Airport. I ate the most delicious and decadent combination of tastes in one ice cream; it was called Cappuccino Commotion, and consisted of coffee ice cream with bits of chocolate, toasted almond and caramel chips. Well, I combined three of those four most complementary tastes in this ice cream, working one of them, the caramel, into a warm sauce to accompany the ice cream. I always reckon that providing you accompany an ice with a warm sauce, you can serve it as a pud twelve months of the year.

SERVES 6–8

4 oz/112 g dark chocolate	*instant coffee granules*
3 large eggs, separated	*dissolved in 2 tbsp boiling*
3 oz/84 g sieved icing sugar	*water, then let it cool*
2 tbsp very strong black-	*½ pt/285 ml double cream,*
coffee – use 1 rounded tsp	*whipped*

Melt the chocolate and pour it on to a sheet of baking parchment on a baking tray. Cool, then break this into bits. It doesn't matter if the bits of chocolate are different sizes.

Whisk the whites till fairly stiff, then, still whisking, gradually add the sieved icing sugar, holding back about 1 tablespoon. When you have a stiff meringue-like mixture, and using the same unwashed whisks, whisk the yolks till thick and pale, with the remaining tablespoon of icing sugar. Whisk the coffee into the yolks. With a large metal spoon fold the yolks mixture into the whipped cream, and then the meringue mixture into the cream with the chocolate.

Pour into a solid container and freeze. There is no need to whip this ice cream during its freezing time, because it doesn't form crystals.

Caramel Sauce

½ pt/285 ml water
6 oz/170 g granulated sugar
2 oz/56 g demerara sugar
4 oz/112 g butter cut into bits

¼ pt/140 ml double cream
A few drops of vanilla
    extract, or ½ tsp essence

Put the water and sugars into a fairly large and heavy-based saucepan, over a moderate heat. Shake the pan gently till the sugars dissolve completely. Be sure that they are dissolved before you let the liquid come to the boil. Boil for 10 minutes. Then take the pan off the heat and whisk in the butter, bit by bit. Lastly, stir in the cream and the vanilla.

Cool, and store in a screw-top jar. Reheat to serve – you will find that the sauce separates in the jar, with the fudgy top and the sugar syrup base. It all comes together on stirring and remains together on reheating. Before serving, boil the sauce for 2 minutes.

Date and Ginger Pudding

This pudding is perfect if it is accompanied by the Warm Caramel Sauce in the previous recipe, and also by crème fraîche, which contrasts deliciously well with the sweetness of the caramel sauce.

The pudding has a very gooey texture, most satisfying for those who love hot puddings. It is simple to make, and it freezes very well.

SERVE 5–6

---

4 oz/112 g chopped dates
¼ pt/140 ml milk
6–8 pieces of stem ginger,
    drained of their syrup
    and chopped

4 oz/112 g flour, sieved
½ tsp bicarbonate of soda
2 tsp cinnamon
1 large egg
2 oz/56 g butter, melted

Put the chopped dates and the milk into a small saucepan and simmer very gently for 5 minutes. Then stir up the contents of the pan and leave them, to cool completely. When cold, mix in the chopped stem ginger. Mix this into the sieved flour, bicarbonate of soda and cinnamon, beating in the egg and the melted butter.

Butter a 3-pint/1.7–litre ovenproof dish, and pour and scrape the date and ginger pudding mixture into it. Bake in a moderate oven, 350°F/180°C/Gas Mark 4 for 40–45 minutes. Serve warm.

Lemon Roulade with Raspberry Cream

This is a convenient pudding in that the roulade has to be made in advance. But it is not just for its convenience that it deserves a place in this chapter, it tastes delicious, which has to be the only reason for ever including any recipe in any book! Its convenience is a bonus. You can substitute blackcurrants, blackberries or sliced strawberries for the raspberries in the recipe. We sometimes spread it with lemon curd, or, in season, with lemon and elderflower curd. In the early months of the year I make it with Seville oranges, instead of lemons. It is really a versatile, useful, but above all delicious pud. It is perfect for a summer lunch party.

SERVES 6–8

5 large eggs, separated	*Sieved icing sugar for*
5 oz/140 g caster sugar	*dusting finished roulade*
Juice of 1 lemon	For the filling:
Grated rind of 2 washed	*1 lb/450 g raspberries*
and dried lemons	*2 oz/56 g caster sugar*
2 oz/56 g sieved ground	*¹/₂ pt/285 ml double cream,*
almonds	*whipped*

Line a baking tray about 12 by 14 inches/30 by 35 cm with baking parchment.

Make the roulade by whisking the yolks with the sugar till the mixture is pale and very thick. Whisk in the lemon juice and the grated rind, and the sieved ground almonds. In a bowl, whisk the whites till they are very stiff, then, using a large metal spoon, fold the whites quickly and thoroughly into the lemon mixture. Pour this into the lined tin and smooth even.

Bake in a moderate oven, 350°F/180°C/Gas Mark 4, till firm to the touch, about 25 minutes. Take it out of the oven, cover with a damp teatowel and leave for several hours.

To fill, fold the raspberries and sugar into the whipped cream. Put a fresh sheet of baking parchment on to a work surface. Tip the roulade face down on to the paper and carefully peel the paper off the back of the roulade. Spoon the raspberry cream over the roulade, as evenly as possible, and roll it up away from you, slipping it from the paper on to a serving plate.

Dust with sieved icing sugar before serving, cut into slices about 1 inch/2.5 cm thick. The cutting is easiest done with a serrated knife.

Tarte aux Fruits – Crème Pâtisserie Pie with Fruits

You can vary the fruits you use according to what you can get!

For the pastry:
3 oz/84 g butter, hard from the fridge, cut into bits
5 oz/140 g flour 1 tbsp icing sugar
½ tsp vanilla essence, or a few drops of vanilla extract
For the crème pâtisserie:
¾ pt/420 ml single cream
4 egg yolks – from large eggs

3 oz/84 g caster sugar
½ tsp vanilla essence, or a few drops of vanilla extract
1 level tsp cornflour
For the fruit and glaze:
A selection of fruit, such as halved strawberries, sliced peaches or nectarines, halved green or black grapes, whole raspberries, halved

apricots – to give a
selection.
Good apricot jam, warmed
and sieved, to brush over
the entire surface – this
may sound

a fiddle but believe me, it
is really worth it as it
gives the finished tart a
most professional
appearance

Put the ingredients for the pastry into a food processor and whiz till the mixture resembles fine crumbs. Pat this firmly around the sides and base of a 9-inch/23-cm flan dish.

Put the dish in the fridge for at least one hour, then bake in a moderate oven, 350°F/180°C/Gas Mark 4, till the pastry is pale golden brown – if the pastry shows signs of slipping down the sides at all as it cooks, press it back up with the back of a metal spoon. The cooking time will take about 20–25 minutes.

Make the crème pâtisserie by beating together all the ingredients well. Either cook over a very low temperature in a thick-bottomed pan, stirring all the time till the cream thickens – this takes some time. Alternatively, put the bowl in a microwave oven on a medium heat setting for 2 minutes. Take it out, whisk well and repeat three times, giving in total 8 minutes' cooking time. The cream should be thickened beautifully. If you are in any doubt, give it another minute's cooking.

Leave the cream to cool in the bowl, then spoon it over the base of the baked pastry case. Arrange the sliced fruit in circles – this is fun. Brush the entire surface with the sieved apricot jam – I mean even the sides of the pastry.

Poached Pears with
Ginger Crème Anglaise

Crème anglaise is really just custard in French, but it is so much nicer than the word 'custard' implies. Crème anglaise is made with, in this case, single cream and egg yolks. It is so quick and easy to make if you have a microwave oven. In this pudding, the peeled pears – this, too, is very easy if you use a potato peeler – are poached, then served with the creamy ginger custard poured over them. Ginger and pears go together so well, and the third thing which complements both extremely well is dark chocolate, which you can grate over the surface.

SERVES 6

6 good pears, each peeled, quartered and cored; slice each quarter into half, giving you 8 pieces to each pear, and cover closely with clingfilm

For the poaching syrup:
2 pts/1.1 l of water
12 oz/340 g granulated sugar
The pared rind of 1 lemon

For the crème anglaise:
4 large egg yolks
2 oz/56 g caster sugar + 1 level tsp cornflour, sieved
1 pt/570 ml single cream
A few drops of vanilla essence or ½ tsp extract
6 pieces of stem ginger, drained of their syrup and chopped finely
Dark chocolate

Put the water, sugar and lemon rind into a fairly large saucepan. Over a moderate heat shake the pan slightly till all the granules of sugar have completely dissolved, then boil the syrup fast for 5 minutes. Then poach the pears gently in the syrup for a further 5 minutes. With a slotted spoon, carefully scoop out the pieces of pear, and put them in a shallow serving dish. Mop up, with absorbent kitchen paper, any syrup which accompanies the pears into the dish.

Beat together the yolks, sugar and cornflour, then beat in the cream. Put the bowl into a microwave oven for 2 minutes on a halfway heat. Then whisk the mixture. Recook for 2 minutes, then whisk again. Recook for a third lot of 2 minutes, and whisk again. You will probably have to give it another minute's cooking – how long exactly the crème anglaise takes to cook depends what material the bowl is made from. It should be as thick as good double cream. Cool.

Stir in the vanilla and the chopped ginger. Pour it over the pears in the serving dish. Grate dark chocolate over the surface – hold the chocolate wrapped in a double thickness of foil, to prevent the warmth from your hand melting the chocolate, and use a potato peeler to get thin curls of chocolate.

Blackberry (or Raspberry) and Lemon Mousse Cake

This amount fills an 8-inch/20-cm springform tin. It is such a useful pudding, ideal for a summer lunch party. It freezes beautifully, and you can serve it with a sauce made from liquidized and sieved blackberries (or raspberries), sweetened with icing sugar. You do have to sieve the purée, both for the mousse part of the cake and for the accompanying sauce, because no liquidizer or food processor has blades that pulverize the tiny woody seeds which stud both fruit.

SERVES 8–10

For the base:
2 large eggs, separated
2½ oz/70 g caster sugar
2 level tbsp plain flour
1 level tbsp ground almonds
2 level tbsp semolina
Grated rind and juice of 1 lemon

For the mousse:
1 lb/450 g blackberries (or raspberries)
2 lemons, their rinds grated and their juices squeezed
1 sachet of gelatine
3 large eggs, separated
4 oz/112 g caster sugar
¼ pt/140 ml double cream, whipped, but not stiffly

Line the base of the tin with a disc of baking parchment, and line the sides of the tin, too, with baking parchment. Don't be tempted to line only the base of the tin – lining the sides as well makes the turning out of the finished mousse cake so very much easier.

Whisk together the yolks and sugar till very thick and pale, till a trail is left and holds its shape on the surface of the mixture. This takes several minutes' whisking. Whisk in the sieved flour, ground almonds and semolina, and the lemon rind and juice. Lastly, with a clean whisk, whisk the whites till very stiff and, with a large metal spoon, fold them quickly and thoroughly through the lemony mixture. Pour and scrape it all into the prepared tin and bake in a moderate oven, 350°F/180°C/Gas Mark 4, for 20 minutes, until firm to the touch.

Cook the blackberries (or raspberries) briefly by putting them into a saucepan – if possible not an aluminium one – over moderate heat just till their juices run. Take the pan off the heat. Put the lemon rinds and juices into a small saucepan and sprinkle in the gelatine. Over a gentle heat shake the pan till the granules have completely dissolved. Take the pan off the heat. Purée the blackberries and gelatine lemon juices, and sieve the purée. Leave in a bowl to cool. If you are in a hurry, put sieved purée in a metal bowl in a washing-up bowl of cold water and ice cubes, stirring the purée till it thickens as it gels. Take the bowl out of the icy water.

In a separate bowl whisk the yolks with the sugar till thick. Fold this into the blackberry purée. Fold in the whipped cream. Lastly, whisk two of the egg whites till stiff, and, with a large metal spoon, fold them through the blackberry mixture. Pour this mousse mixture on top of the baked lemony cake base, and leave to set. Cover with clingfilm.

To serve, unmould the mousse cake from its tin on to a serving plate. Decorate with fresh blackberries (or raspberries) around the base of the cake, on the plate. Serve with the accompanying sauce if you like – it does look pretty.

Strawberry and Cinnamon Meringue Bombe

Cinnamon goes so well with a variety of soft summer fruits, but especially with strawberries and raspberries – you can use raspberries instead of strawberries for this recipe. If you like, make a jewel-coloured sauce to accompany the bombe, by whizzing strawberries, or raspberries, in the food processor with icing sugar, then sieving the purée. This freezes very well. I like to put the bombe mixture into a clingfilm-lined loaf tin. It is very easy to slice neatly for serving, and also very easy to turn out. The recipe is simplicity itself, but the taste is awfully good.

SERVES 6–8

3 large egg whites	*1 lb/450 g strawberries,*
6 oz/170 g caster sugar	*whizzed briefly – to break*
2 tsp powdered cinnamon	*them up rather than*
½ pt/285 ml whipped	*purée them*
cream	

Line a baking tray with a sheet of baking parchment. In a clean bowl whisk the egg whites till they are stiff then, whisking all the time, gradually add the sugar, sprinkling it in with the whites a spoonful at a time. When all the sugar is incorporated, with a large metal spoon, briefly fold in the cinnamon. Spoon even-sized dollops of the meringue mixture on to the baking parchment.

Bake in a cool oven, 250°F/130°C/Gas Mark ½, for about 3 hours – they should lift easily off the paper. When they are cooked and cooled, crunch them in your hands and fold them into the whipped cream with the processed strawberries. Line a 2-lb/900-g loaf tin, or Pyrex terrine mould, with clingfilm, and spoon and scrape the mixture into the lined terrine. Press it down well. Freeze it. When it is frozen cover the top with clingfilm.

To turn out, bring the terrine into room temperature for 10 minutes, then dip the tin in hot water. Turn on to a serving plate and peel off the clingfilm. Decorate, if you like, with strawberries with their stalks left on, and with strawberry leaves if you grow your own strawberries – strawberries in themselves and their leaves are as decorative as I could possibly wish for. Slice the bombe and serve it, if you like, with sieved puréed strawberries sweetened with icing sugar. This makes a most perfect summer-time pud.

Chocolate and Ginger Meringue Bombe

This is a winter version of the Strawberry and Cinnamon meringue bombe, but of course you can make it at any time of the year! Chocolate and ginger go together so very well. Because of the meringue content this bombe is easily sliced. I like to make it in a clingfilm-lined loaf tin or terrine tin, but if you prefer you could put it to freeze in a pudding bowl lined with clingfilm. If you really want to 'gild the lily' – as I do – you can make a dark chocolate sauce to accompany the meringue bombe.

SERVES 6–8

3 large egg whites
6 oz/170 g caster sugar
A few drops vanilla extract
1/2 pt/285 ml whipped
  cream
4 oz/112 g best dark
  chocolate, grated

6–8 pieces of stem ginger,
  drained of their
  preserving syrup, and
  chopped quite finely

Line a baking tray with a sheet of baking parchment. In a clean bowl whisk the whites till they are stiff, then, whisking all the time, gradually sprinkle in the sugar, a spoonful at a time and whisking well between each spoonful. When it is all incorporated, briefly whisk in the vanilla. With a metal spoon, put even-sized dollops of meringue on to the prepared baking tray and bake in a cool oven, 250°F/130°C/Gas Mark 1/2, for 2 1/2–3 hours – the meringues should lift off the paper when they are cooked. Cool them, then scrunch them in your hand.

Fold together the crushed meringues, whipped cream, grated

dark chocolate and ginger. Pack this stiff mixture into the lined tin and freeze. When frozen, cover with clingfilm and put it back in the freezer.

Before serving, take the tin into room temperature for 10 minutes. Dip the tin briefly in very hot water, turn it on to a serving plate and peel off the clingfilm. Slice to serve.

Dark Chocolate Soufflés

This is one of my favourite of all puddings, provided the chocolate is the best. We buy a Belgian chocolate called Callebaut, and I like it the best of all the very many chocolates I have tasted. These are simple to make, but they must be eaten as soon as they emerge from the oven. That is why I have discovered that they cook perfectly in a moderate oven for 25 minutes, which allows you to put them into the oven as you serve the main course – 25 minutes seems about the right time from then till pudding! Serve them with plain whipped cream, cold from the fridge.

SERVES 8

8 oz/225 g of the best dark chocolate, broken into bits	*A few drops vanilla extract, or ½ tsp vanilla essence*
½ pt/285 ml single cream + 2 tsp caster sugar	*5 large eggs, separated*

Butter 8 ramekins and dust each one with caster sugar. Put them into a baking tray with an inch/2.5 cm of water in the tray. Melt the chocolate in the cream and leave till quite cold. Beat in the vanilla, sugar and the egg yolks, one by one and beating well. In a clean bowl whisk the whites till stiff and, with a large metal spoon, fold them quickly and thoroughly through the chocolate mixture. Divide this between the prepared ramekins and put the tray into a moderate oven, 350°F/180°C/Gas Mark 4, for 25 minutes.

Dust each soufflé with sieved icing sugar before serving them, accompanied by a bowl of whipped cream. Have the sieve, icing sugar and a spoon ready, as well as small plates on which to sit the ramekins once the soufflés' cooking time is up, so as to take as little time as possible getting them to the table and your guests.

Lemon and Vanilla Soufflés

I love the combined flavours of lemon and vanilla. These soufflés make delicious eating for a special lunch-time pudding. They are convenient to prepare because you can make them in their entirety, including folding in the whisked whites, then cover the whole lot with clingfilm, get washed up, and leave the soufflés for a couple of hours. Whip off the clingfilm before putting them into the oven to cook. But, as with all soufflés, they must then be eaten immediately – dust with icing sugar, which you have all ready with the spoon and sieve!

FILLS 6 LARGE RAMEKINS

5 large eggs, separated	*A few drops of vanilla*
5 oz/170 g caster sugar	*extract, or ½ tsp essence*
Grated rind of 2 well	*2 oz/56 g ground almonds,*
washed and dried lemons	*sieved*
Juice of 1 lemon	*Butter and icing sugar*

Butter the ramekins and dust them out with icing sugar.

Whisk the egg yolks, gradually adding the sugar and whisking till the mousse-like mixture is very pale and thick. Whisk in the lemon rinds and juice, the vanilla and the ground almonds. In a separate bowl, with clean whisks, whisk the whites till they are stiff. With a large metal spoon fold them quickly and thoroughly through the lemon mixture. Divide evenly between the prepared ramekins. Bake in a moderate oven, 350°F/180°C/Gas Mark 4, for 25 minutes.

Dust each with icing sugar and serve immediately, with a bowl of whipped cream, or with a sieved raspberry purée if you prefer. Or with both.

Pear and Almond Glazed Tarts

You can prepare this pud well in advance – you can even bake them and reheat them, but they are nicest baked then eaten. However, you can do all the messy work and get everything washed up in advance so I don't see much point pre-baking the individual tarts anyway. It is such a help being able to buy ready-rolled out puff pastry. This is an ideal pud to make in the autumn, when pears are in the natural season. You need firm pears, not too ripe.

SERVES 6

Ready rolled out puff pastry, cut into 6 oblong shapes, each approx. 3 inches by 2 inches/7.5 by 5 cm

3 good-sized pears, round rather than the elongated shape of Conference pears

4 oz/112 g ground almonds

1 oz/28 g caster sugar

Grated rind of 1 washed and dried lemon

Juice of half a lemon

A very few drops of almond extract – not, if at all possible, essence

2 oz/56 g butter, melted

3 tbsp caster sugar

Put the pastry oblongs on to a baking tray – no need to butter the baking tray. With a potato peeler, peel the pears, cut each in half and scoop out the core. In a bowl mix together the ground almonds, 1 oz/28 g sugar, grated lemon rind and juice and the almond extract and, using your hand, mix together. The warmth of your hand and the lemon juice will combine to bind together the mixture into an almond paste. Divide this almond paste between each pastry oblong and put a pear half on top. Brush each oblong of pastry and pear half all over with melted butter, then sprinkle each with caster sugar.

Cover closely with clingfilm till you are ready to pop the tray into the oven. Bake in a hot oven, 400°F/200°C/Gas Mark 6, till the pastry is puffed and golden and the pear is just turning golden. Serve warm, with crème anglaise on page 218.

Baked Nectarine, Raspberry and Cinnamon Pudding

You can substitute peaches for the nectarines in this pudding if you prefer. It is just as good made with either fruit. Cinnamon is a most versatile spice, and it complements the flavour of most summer soft fruits. Nectarines and peaches are no exception. I like to serve good vanilla ice cream with this.

SERVE 6

8 nectarines	1 tsp baking powder
6 oz/170 g soft brown sugar	1 tbsp caster sugar
1 level tbsp cornflour	4 oz/112 g butter, cut into
Juice of 1 lemon	bits, hard from the fridge
2 oz/56 g butter	2 tsp cinnamon powder
6 oz/170 g raspberries	A few drops of vanilla
For the topping:	extract, or ½ tsp essence
8 oz/225 g plain flour	

Skin the nectarines by boiling water in a saucepan and sticking each nectarine, impaled on a fork, into boiling water for a few seconds. The skins should then peel off easily. Chop the flesh and throw the stones away.

In a saucepan mix together the chopped nectarines, sugar, cornflour, lemon juice, butter and raspberries. Over a gentle heat stir all together till the butter melts, the raspberries seep their juice, and the mixture thickens. Then put this into an ovenproof dish.

Make the top by whizzing together all the ingredients in a food processor till the mixture resembles fine breadcrumbs. Cover the top of the fruit, evenly, with this spiced mixture.

Bake in a moderate oven, 350°F/180°C/Gas Mark 4, till the surface is light brown and the fruit is bubbling around the edges – about 25 minutes. Serve warm. It reheats well.

Puffed Chocolate Chip and Pecan Biscuits

You can vary the nut content of these delicious biscuits – use chopped almonds, or walnuts if you prefer, instead of the pecans, but these days it is easy to find pecan nuts in the shops and those are the nuts I like best for these biscuits. I like to use dark chocolate chips, but if you would rather have milk chocolate, use that instead. They make a really good pud for a children's lunch, but I find that age isn't really a barrier for the pleasure in eating them! This amount makes about 24 biscuits, depending a bit on their size.

8 oz/225 g chopped pecan nuts	*5 oz/140 g butter*
1 oz/28 g butter	*5 oz/140 g soft light brown sugar*
12 oz/340 g plain flour	*1 large egg*
½ tsp salt	*1 tsp vanilla extract*
1½ tsp baking powder	*8 oz/225 g dark chocolate chips*

Put the nuts into a wide-based saucepan and dry fry for several minutes to refresh their flavour. Then take the pan off the heat and stir the 1 oz/28 g of butter into the hot nuts, mixing it in well. Sieve together the flour, salt and baking powder. In another bowl beat the butter and sugar together till almost fluffy. Beat in the egg, beating thoroughly (I use a hand-held electric whisk for all this beating). Beat in the vanilla. Gradually beat in the sieved dry ingredients, mixing all very well. Stir in the chopped nuts and chocolate chips.

Lightly oil baking trays – you will probably need two, depending on their size. Put tablespoons of dough, well spaced, on the baking trays. Bake for 12 minutes – their edges should just be turning golden brown. Leave them for a minute on their baking trays before carefully lifting them off with a spatula, on to a wire cooling rack. Leave till cooled.

If you would like more biscuits, make them smaller by putting teaspoons of the dough on to the baking trays, but when they are to be served as a pudding for lunch, they are better on the larger side.

Lime and Mango Sorbet with Mango Salad and Lime

Mangoes are so easy to buy these days. I even found some perfectly ripe ones in the Co-op in Broadford, our local town here on Skye. They make a delicious sorbet, refreshing, yet with more substance to it than lemon sorbet, for instance. Accompany the sorbet by chopped mangoes (it is pretty well impossible to slice a mango neatly without wasting at least half of the fruit) with lime juice squeezed over them which just sharpens up the taste of the whole.

SERVES 6–8

1 pt/570 ml water
6 oz/170 g granulated sugar
Pared rind of 2 limes and
    their juice
2 mangoes, pared of their
    skin and flesh chopped
    from the stones

For the salad:
4 mangoes, skin pared off
    and the flesh chopped as
    neatly as possible
Juice of 2 limes

Put the water and sugar into a saucepan with the pared lime rinds. Over a moderate heat shake the pan or stir from time to time, till the grains of sugar have completely dissolved. Then, and only then, let the liquid come to the boil. Boil for 5 minutes, then draw the pan off the heat and stir in the lime juice. Let this cool. When it is cold, fish out the strips of lime rind and whiz in a liquidizer or food processor, with the mango flesh. If you have an ice cream making machine, freeze and churn the mixture in it till it is a soft smooth and thick frozen sorbet. Freeze it in a solid container. If you don't have a machine, freeze the purée in a shallow container.

When you remember, chip the frozen sorbet (which will have the texture of ice lollies) into a food processor and whiz. Refreeze this slush. Repeat this three more times – if over a period of days; it doesn't matter a bit refreezing semi-thawed ices such as this one, because it has no dairy produce in it. By whizzing the sorbet in the processor like this you improve the texture so much that you will be able, after four whizzings, to spoon the sorbet from the freezer.

For the accompanying salad, just put the chopped mango flesh into a pretty dish and pour over the lime juice.

Bread and Butter Pudding with Cream and Nutmeg

This a ritzy version of the old nursery favourite – of some. But this version, I have found, appeals to just about everyone. The bread is rich, there are no hard chunks of peel because any peel is soft, within the bread. Yet there is a distinct but subtle citrus flavour with the grated orange and lemon rinds. It is soft and creamy in texture.

SERVES 6–8

12 slices of malt loaf (the sort with peel and raisins in it, preferably), each slice buttered and cut in half	*2 oz/56 g caster sugar*
	A good grating of nutmeg
	Grated rind of ½ lemon and ½ orange
¾ pint/420 ml single cream	*1 rounded tbsp demerara sugar*
1 whole egg + 2 large egg yolks	*Butter*

Butter an ovenproof dish. Arrange the sliced buttered bits of malt bread in the dish. In a bowl beat together the cream, egg and yolks, caster sugar, nutmeg and lemon and orange rinds. Pour this over the malt bread, and sprinkle the surface with demerara sugar, as evenly as possible. Bake in a moderate oven, 350°F/180°C/Gas Mark 4, for about 20 minutes, or until the nutmeg custard is just set. Serve warm.

Fudge Brownie Pie with Vanilla Ice Cream

This is my idea of a heavenly pud for lunch on a Saturday or Sunday. It smacks to me of the type of pud more suited to kitchen informality than the dining room. If you like, you can gild the already well-adorned (in this case) lily by serving Warm Caramel Sauce (see page 214) with this gooey warm brownie pie and the ice cream.

SERVES 6

4 oz/112 g good-quality (it goes without saying) dark chocolate, broken into bits	*¼ tsp baking powder*
	4 oz/112 g butter
	6 oz/170 g soft brown sugar
2 oz/56 g self-raising flour	*1 large egg + 1 egg yolk*
2 tbsp cocoa powder (not drinking chocolate!)	*1 tsp vanilla extract*

Put the broken-up chocolate into a bowl over (but not touching) a saucepan of gently simmering water. Let the chocolate melt, then take the bowl off the heat.

Butter a 9-inch/23-cm pie plate or metal flan dish. Sieve together the flour, cocoa and baking powder. Beat the butter, gradually adding the sugar, and beat very well. Beat in the egg and yolk, and beat in the vanilla, beating all very well. Beat in the melted chocolate, then fold in the sieved ingredients. Scrape this mixture into the buttered pie or flan dish and spread it evenly.

Bake in a moderate oven, 350°F/180°C/Gas Mark 4, for 25–30 minutes – a skewer should come out sticky when pushed into the centre of the pudding. Serve warm, cut into wedges.

Vanilla Ice Cream

This is the recipe I like best. It tastes good, has an excellent texture, and doesn't need beating at half frozen.

SERVES 6–8

4 large eggs, separated	*½ pt/285 ml double cream,*
4 oz/112 g sieved icing sugar	*whipped, but not too*
A few drops of vanilla extract, or ½ tsp essence	*stiffly*

Whisk the egg whites till they are fairly stiff, then, whisking continuously, gradually add all but about 1 tablespoon of the sieved icing sugar, whisking till you have a stiff meringue. There is no need to wash the whisks, go straight on and whisk the yolks, adding the remainder of the icing sugar, and whisking till you have a thick and pale mixture. Whisk in the vanilla. With a large metal spoon, fold the yolks and cream together, then fold in the meringue mixture. Freeze this in a solid container.

Take the container out of the freezer and into room temperature for 20 minutes before serving.

Lemon Crumble Cake

Of course (because I am so weak-willed) I will eat cake at any time, but I know many people who think it is really sinful to indulge in cake eating at teatime, yet their consciences will permit them to eat cake when they are served it for a pudding. Lemon Crumble Cake fits perfectly into the pudding category for the finale to a Saturday lunch. If you like, you can serve it warm, when it will be slightly more crumbly, with crème fraîche.

SERVES 6–8

12 oz/340 g self-raising flour	*1 large egg*
8 oz/225 g caster sugar	*1 tsp vanilla essence, or ½*
Finely grated rind of 2 well	*tsp extract*
washed and dried lemons	*1 tsp baking powder*
½ tsp powdered cinnamon	*1 tsp bicarbonate of soda*
¼ pt/140 ml sunflower oil	*Icing sugar, to sieve over*
2 tbsp lemon juice	*the surface of the finished*
½ pt/285 ml sour cream or	*cake*
crème fraîche	

Line an 8-inch/20-cm square cake tin with baking parchment.

Sieve the flour into a bowl and mix in the sugar, grated lemon rinds and cinnamon. Stir in the oil and lemon juice and mix well –

the mixture will clog up in lumps. Put a quarter of the mixture on one side. Whisk together the sour cream or crème fraîche, the egg, vanilla, baking powder and bicarbonate of soda until really well mixed. Beat this into the crumb mixture, mixing all until smooth. Scrape this into the lined cake tin. Sprinkle the reserved crumb mixture over the surface.

Bake in a moderate oven, 350°F/180°C/Gas Mark 4, for 35–40 minutes – when you stick a skewer into the middle it should come out clean. Sieve icing sugar over the surface whilst still hot. Cool in the tin. Cut in squares to serve.

Index

INDEX